Stories from Schools

Stories from Schools

*Case Studies of the California
Academic Partnership Program*

EDITED BY
Alice Kawazoe

CALIFORNIA ACADEMIC
PARTNERSHIP PROGRAM
Long Beach, California

DISTRIBUTED IN ASSOCIATION WITH
University of California Press
Berkeley   Los Angeles   London

ISBN 978-0-615-27731-8

Cover Design: Barry Tao
Cover Photography: Van Nguyen, Overfelt High School
Interior Design and Composition: BookMatters

The California Academic Partnership Program is
an intersegmental program supporting partnerships
between K-12 and postsecondary institutions designed
to close the achievement gap and improve college-
going rates for students in the state's underperforming
schools. CAPP is administered by the California State
University, in cooperation with the Association of
Independent Colleges and Universities, California
Community Colleges, California Department of
Education, California Postsecondary Education
Commission, California Student Aid Commission, and
University of California.

For more information about CAPP:
Visit our Web site: www.calstate.edu/capp
Call: 562-951-4780
Write: California Academic Partnership Program
CSU Chancellor's Office, 401 Golden Shore, 6th Floor
Long Beach, CA 90802

Contents

Acknowledgments

The California Academic Partnership Program (CAPP) would like to extend our sincere appreciation to all of the educators who have been part of our programs. Without the many teachers, administrators, and staff who work in the CAPP schools there would be no partnership. We appreciate your dedication and commitment to educating all students and contributing to our knowledge about teaching, learning, and leadership.

We especially thank all of the Case Study authors for sharing with us your expertise and insights about your important work with the students, teachers, and others. The writers of the commentaries deserve our thanks for providing additional perspectives and insights about the work described in the case studies.

The CAPP Advisory Board has provided sustained support throughout this endeavor. The Advisory Board represents all of the educational segments in California—Lawton Gray and Terry McAteer (Californa Public Schools); Penni Hansen (California Department of Education); Michelle Kalina and Jeff Spano (California Community Colleges); Jacinta Amaral, Roberta Ching and Lorie Roth (California State University); Ruth Cossey (Independent Colleges and Universities); Jorge Aguilar, Robert Cooper, and Nina Moore (University of California); Karen Humphrey (California Postsecondary Education Commission); and Linda Doughty (Student Aid Commision—Cal-SOAP). We also appreciate Dave Jolly, Eleanor Knott and Virginia Soto from the California State University Chancellor's Office for providing a home and administrative support for CAPP.

Finally, a special thanks to Janice Agee for her help with editing the case studies and commentaries. Her keen eyes and sharpened pencil improved our prose.

Introduction

ALICE KAWAZOE

WHY STORIES AND CASE STUDIES?

My father was a noted surgeon, loved by his patients, respected by his colleagues, revered by his students. I once asked him what made him such a good doctor and teacher. He shrugged his shoulders as if to say, "Who knows?" But then he thought a bit and gave a simple and surprisingly unsurgeonlike answer: "I'm a good listener. We all carry stories with us on this journey we take together—patient and doctor, student and teacher. Science tells one kind of story, but our patients and students tell us more important human stories. We owe it to each other to listen to our stories, to respect and learn from them. Our stories are all we have."

The California Academic Partnership Program (CAPP) has, for 20 years, supported efforts of teachers and schools to improve student achievement in secondary schools. In the last six years, CAPP has focused its efforts on the challenges of teaching and learning in California's lowest performing high schools, confronting head-on the issues of equity and access, high expectations, and rigorous instruction for all students.

Why focus on high schools? Because they are difficult, complex places to understand and change. Disengagement that may have sprouted in middle or junior high school takes root firmly in high school. Disconnection, both academic and social, proliferates and deepens. Support systems dissolve, lose effectiveness, or lose their funding.

In a large high school, more students "fall through the cracks," as the cracks become canyons. Parent participation falls away, and the strong ties of communication and involvement that bound together school, teacher, parent/caregiver, and the community in elementary school begin to fray in middle school, and unravel in high school.

A great strength of CAPP is that its work resides in schools. CAPP recognizes that the action, if there is to be action, happens in classrooms—not at a federal or state agency or department, not in a professor's seminar, not in the superintendent's or the principal's office, but in real, not virtual, classrooms, filled with learners, lively to inert, led by teachers, bold to jaded.

We have much documentation about each school involved in CAPP initiatives. Each school is evaluated annually by the research division of WestEd; pertinent data are collected; and project directors file reports, registering successes and challenges and detailing how the CAPP funds have been used. At semi-annual conferences "CAPP schools" from throughout California meet to share their experiences, learn from one another, problem-solve, and plan. But what happens at each school unfolds as an unending narrative, a story, with a complex plot and subplots, a spectrum of characters, multiple motives, high and low points. As with a story, the work of a school can never be charted as a straight line progression or ascension. That would not only be boring, but unreal. Change in schools happens in fits and starts; progress gets derailed; "the best laid plans" remain as plans or become unplanned; and sometimes pleasant or unpleasant surprises pop up.

We want to tell some of these school stories, told by people in the school—teachers, project directors, and CAPP consultants. These stories, once written, become case studies that we can then discuss, comment upon, analyze, and argue about. These are not formal, academic case studies (although some are more formal than others), but a retelling of an experience or description of a project, imbued with the teller's personal voice.

Some readers may become impatient and will want to rush to conclusions. But the whole point of stories and case studies is not "solutions" or "resolutions," but a broadening and even a heightening of our struggles—with new protagonists and antagonists introduced, with new sources of concern or apprehension or hope. A story or case study does not necessarily provide an easy answer or a happy ending. But it may prompt a kind of collaborative thinking, not in the sense of a "let's put our minds together" group brainstorm, but that kind of response a skilled kindergarten teacher elicits from each child after asking the whole group, "What did you think of that story?" A good story or case study should cause conversation, an occasion to talk to one another about issues that matter. And the case studies should teach us some truths about teaching and learning, about teacher and administrative leadership, about how to make schools a better place for all students. The power is in the storytelling, and as my father said, "We owe it to each other to listen to our stories, to respect and learn from them."

That the case studies are embedded in classrooms and centered on the struggles of teachers and their students is critically important at this time. Any number of "school reformers" are promoting quick fixes with fast, but not lasting results, "teacher-proof" instructional materials, and one-time inservice training, validating the inoculation theory of professional development: one shot will cure the diseased teacher for at least a year. One-answer, context-less solutions delivered by transient consultants who briefly appear at the school or by change agents who insist that everyone see the problem in the same way are the bane of desperate schools.

Struggling high schools are weary of "being done to" by outsiders. High schools must gain the capacity to do things for themselves and base their doings on sound decisions. Some of their most important decisions must be informed by theory and not be the consequence solely of opinions, preferences, or feelings. But teacher-practitioners often distrust or resent theoreticians who, some teachers think, research and write, uncontaminated by reality, while the teachers are "fighting in the trenches." Theoreticians do not help their cause by writing long tracts, densely footnoted, in impenetrable language, to an audience of other theoreticians who write like they do. Most practicing teachers, unless they are doctoral candidates, do not have the time or mental energy to plod through such writing. Practitioners like what is "useful," "practical," "useable," "pragmatic," not what is "abstract," "theoretical," "densely footnoted," or "impenetrable." I've seen eyes roll back and heard audible groans at the mere mention of the word "research-based."

However, this opposition of theory versus practice is in many ways false. Teachers forget, or *they do not have the opportunity to realize,* that they are the theory and that their practice is the "being in reality" of their theory. Some teachers may have difficulty articulating their teaching theory. Some have not yet developed philosophical and pedagogical beliefs and values. Others have not challenged or leaned against their beliefs in a long time. Though they automatically assign research papers to their students, rarely do teachers formulate research questions about their teaching, probe that question in their classroom, and examine their findings. Yet thoughtful teachers are plagued by uncertainties and questions about their teaching. Does homework improve class work? Why did third period do so much better on the assignment than fourth period? Does teaching U.S. history chronologically develop an understanding of historical time? Why did the English learners do better on this assignment than the English speakers? Does note taking promote comprehension? What do I do when most of my students cannot read or understand the text?

But teachers are not taught how to frame their uncertainties as research questions or shown how to pursue informal research in their classrooms or even to test some of their instructional assumptions and practices. Sound research, cogently written, can help bridge the gap between theory and application for teachers, may illuminate an issue, may compel teachers to examine their beliefs, or at the very least, give them the opportunity to look at an old problem in a new way. But at many high schools, teachers do not have the time to read research or think critically about their teaching, engage in systematic lesson study, problem solve individually or collaboratively, or even talk to one another about teaching and learning. Ideally, the classroom is where theory and practice intersect. In reality, the classroom is rarely seen as a learning place for teachers.

However, these case studies show that some effective teachers have crossed the bridge between practice and theory, not just on the knowledge constructed by theorists and researchers, but also on the knowledge constructed from their own wisdom of practice. In analyzing the literal meaning of the word "theory," I learned that a critical root is the Greek *theamai,* "I behold," as in what we see when we go to the theater. We hold something visual in our minds; theory, then, is an enlargement of observation. In these case studies, we observe teachers testing their pedagogical theory and questioning their practice. We see them trying to build community so that they can trust each other enough to take risks. We see teachers taking leadership and administrators re-envisioning their roles. And we see struggle because little of this work is easy or tidy. Distractions and opposition abound, and forces continually conspire to isolate teachers and muffle dialogue. By linking theory to practice, these case studies magnify the images and sounds of real, live students and teachers in classrooms and enable us to "behold" the realities and struggles revealed there. We don't behold with abstract treatises. We do not behold with a systematic exposition of ideas. We behold with a story, because in a story, as it says in the Gospel of John, *"the word becomes flesh."*

RECURRING THEMES

As we read these case studies, some recurring themes or topics emerge and reverberate as the writers probe factors that enable or disable their efforts for school improvement. Some cases will discuss a theme directly; in others the theme is subtext, moving just below the surface of the narrative. Not all themes are discussed in a case, but at least one of the themes becomes prominent in each case.

All schools in these cases are grappling with issues of *leadership.* What is leadership? Who are the leaders? How is leadership developed? What's to be done in the absence of effective leadership? Some schools recognize the critical need to develop *professional community* and a culture of trust and responsibility so that the school can confront difficult issues and ask hard questions of itself. Because the business of schools is teaching and learning, the major issues confronting the schools inevitably involve *curriculum, instruction, and assessment,* and teachers recognize the necessity for *student support,* but they are struggling with how to make support services most effective and serve all students who need help. Fundamental to all these themes is *professional development* and the need to redefine what it means because professional development is the agent for change and improvement in all other areas. A short discussion of each of these themes follows.

Leadership

Much research focuses on the critical role of administrative leadership in the development of a dynamic professional culture leading to whole school improvement. Strong administrators usually have a clear vision for the school—where it is, where it should be, where it is heading—and they know how to marshall resources and more importantly, win the hearts and minds of the staff to get there. Administrators without these skills should at least recognize that one form of minimal support is to stay out of the way and not unwittingly obstruct a well-conceived and planned improvement effort. We will not discuss here administrators who exercise powerful "negative leadership" by actively undermining or overtly or covertly opposing improvement efforts, other than to say ruefully that they exist, and they do harm.

One administrator, however effective and charismatic, cannot change a high school. Widespread improvement in a school requires teacher leaders. Teacher leaders may already thrive in formalized roles—department chair, leadership team or other decision-making group, coach, teacher on special assignment—or "untitled" teachers may emerge as leaders due to their expertise, experience, and the respect of their colleagues. Administrators may lead the development of a professional culture focused on improved instruction, but teacher leaders with content and pedagogical knowledge are necessary to influence groups of teachers and gain their trust and effect improved instruction in classrooms. An administrator would be wise to invest in the development of teacher leaders and allocate resources to support their work (i.e., coaching training, release time). Further, this combination of administrator and teacher leadership greatly facilitates the development of a professional community.

Professional Community

High schools are hard places. High school staffs are hard audiences. Think of a fairly large group of 50 to 120 adults—generally nice, but not docile, opinionated, strong-willed, diverse in beliefs and values. On one end of the spectrum, when confronted with a new initiative, program, or mandate, the youthful novice, eager, but overwhelmed, sinks beneath "yet another thing on top of everything else"; on the other extreme, the jaded veteran kicks back, confident that, like the plague, "this, too, shall pass." Somewhere in between are the Garbo isolates, who want only to shut their doors and be left alone. Hopefully, some peppy teachers still remain with enough energy and hope to try something.

This broad-brush characterization does not accurately describe all high schools staffs, but there is enough truth here to underscore the difficulties of creating a professional community in a high school. However, we rest our hope on the belief that the vast majority of teachers at a school share a common goal: to make their school a better place of learning for all their students and themselves. Teachers yearn for *solidarity of purpose,* rather than dispersion of efforts in different directions. Most teachers would prefer *colleagues* to strangers on the other side of the classroom walls. But transforming strangers into colleagues requires interaction—conversation, building relationships, acts of support, what one teacher describes as "the comfort to criticize," and meaningful acts of collaboration, of working together. Eating, drinking, and socializing together certainly help to stimulate community; however, a professional community requires more than congeniality. A professional community creates a culture that nurtures risk taking and risk takers and fosters a shared responsibility for actions. A professional community builds trust, welcomes discussion, considers debate healthy, and continually tests the efficacy of its decisions. Put bluntly, a professional community manifests the vital signs of a living organism, not an inanimate object. No one wants to be at an inanimate school.

Curriculum, Instruction, and Assessment

A school may spend a good amount of time building a professional community, but sooner or later (hopefully sooner), the school must turn its attention to teaching and learning. To confront seriously and honestly the issues of equity and access, high expectations, and rigorous instruction for all students is a daunting challenge for high schools. The evidence that a school is meeting this challenge is not in documents—courses of study, the school plan, the master schedule—but in classrooms. We need to go into classrooms, observe instruction, and look at student work to discover that sometimes different versions of a curriculum are offered to different classes and that performance expectations are adjusted for marginalized students. Not all students may be asked to produce work that requires higher-order thinking, and not all teachers conceive or design demanding assignments. Importantly, a school may be unintentionally practicing a kind of informal tracking, by grouping students in classes based on the need for "remediation."

As mentioned previously, teachers are plagued by uncertainties and questions about their teaching that puzzle and confound them. They learn to live with dissonance—the discord between teacher expectations and student performance, between what they are trying to teach and what students learn, between what they want of themselves and what they are able to do. This constant dissonance and "dis-ease" may prompt teachers to reevaluate their notions about teaching and learning and may lead the school to examine its educational assumptions and practices.

In many schools, contending seriously and honestly with the complex issues of curriculum, instruction, and assessment will require fundamental changes in deeply held beliefs about schooling and students and will demand *transformative changes* to the status quo.

Student Support

Discussions about student support are wide-ranging and might include counselors; career guidance; college/university connections; transition or bridge activites with middle schools; advisory/homeroom periods; teacher-advisors; peer counseling; sustained silent reading; remediation classes; use of aides and teaching assistants; study halls; peer, cross-age, and teacher-led tutoring (in class, before, and after school); after-school programs; homework clubs; buddy systems; Saturday School; and summer school. Schools are trying to offer the most appropriate combination of services to reach all students who need additional help, extensive and intensive academic support, guidance, and advice.

Tutoring has become a particularly problematic issue. Although most schools acknowledge that tutoring provides the opportunity for one-on-one assistance and targeted help, schools are struggling with how best to structure the services, who should tutor, when to tutor, training for tutors, and engaging all students who would benefit from the services.

To address the demands of state assessments and the California High School Exit Exam, many schools have designed and instituted support classes to help students gain and advance their academic skills in mathematics and English and enhance their test-taking skills. Many schools hurriedly implemented these classes with little attention to course content, instructional materials, or sound pedagogical practices. Some schools are continuing down this path of "institutionalized remediation," while others now are stepping back and evaluating the efficacy of these classes and trying to determine if there are better ways to meet the learning needs of students.

Professional Development

Given the difficulties of instituting change in high schools, given the imperatives of improving instruction and student achievement, given the challenges to effective teaching and learning in "underperforming schools," given increasing budgetary constraints—the notion of professional development demands bold rethinking and redefinition. An inspiring speaker or a practical workshop may motivate the staff or stimulate thinking, but what kind of professional development will activate and sustain change in curriculum, instruction, and assessment, develop professional community, promote leadership, and strengthen student support and parent and community involvement? Where does a school first concentrate its efforts? What kind of professional development will change instruction in classrooms? How do we ensure that the professional development gets translated into practice? If we value collaboration, how do we build in time for collaborative planning? How might we convert staff meetings into professional development? Who should lead and organize the professional development? How do we fund professional development and teacher time? What about accountabilty as related to professional development? Time is always an issue at high schools. How do we garner, buy, or seize time for professional development? These—and more—are all critical questions that must be answered if systemic change is to become a reality.

THE CASE STUDIES

In "Expect Success: Interventions Beyond Remediation," Katrine Czajkowski discusses four projects—common assessments in mathematics, a tutoring and homework center, summer school acceleration classes, and grade recovery—to build student academic success. Dorothy Russo takes us into an English learner class as she leads her students through a challenging and engaging project involving writing, artwork, and oral presentation. Deep conversations–opportunities to examine and change teaching and learning, address the needs of students, and improve instruction–are critical to reinventing high schools according to Nina Moore in her case study. Barbara Wells's journal helps us understand the uneven path that multi-leveled coaching in mathematics takes. In Ed Landesman's case study, we learn that a concerted, collaborative effort among high schools, higher education, and industry can produce more able science and math students. Kate Jamentz presents the theoretical basis of the Instructional Leadership Initiative and details the application of this standards-based instruction and assessment design process in schools. And in "Women of Color Leading Schools: The Journey of Three Principals," three passionate female educational leaders explain the challenges of high school leadership and reveal their own personal and professional journeys.

What do these case studies, these stories, tell us? They tell us that the struggles and troubles of high schools are real and persistent. But they also show us the passion, commitment, and moral purpose of educators determined to make high schools a better place for students and learning.

"I Liked It Because I Did It"

When Students Find Success

DOROTHY RUSSO

IN THIS CASE STUDY, Dorothy Russo introduces us to her English language development students. She resurrects a unit from her early teaching days and guides these beginning English learners through challenging lessons that ask students to recall a childhood memory and discuss the details of that memory, focusing on the sense most closely connected to the memory. The students then write a reflective essay, create a painting of the memory, and finally give an oral presentation to the whole class describing the painting and reading their reflections. Russo shows that beginning English learners benefit from and deserve lessons that demand complex thinking and integrated reading, writing, and speaking skills, combined with artistic expression.

❖ ❖ ❖

When Julio, Jorge, and Pablo (not their actual names) arrive to work on their final projects, it is 7:30 in the morning. The first bell won't ring for another 30 minutes, yet these students, who are normally late to class, are early and eager to get a head start. Julio wants to make sure the color he used the previous day on his painting of his family's home in Manalisco, Mexico, dried to match the color of the memory that he holds in his heart. Jorge, standing before his painting of the ranch where he spent his childhood, compares it to a tattered photograph he brought from home. And Pablo, after a sleepy, "Hello, Miss," trudges over to his painting taped to the file cabinet by the far window to ensure that it hasn't been marred by one of the more than one hundred students who come through my classroom each day.

Julio, Jorge, and Pablo are three of the eighteen students in my English language development (ELD) level-two class. The class meets daily for 90 minutes from late August to mid-June. All of the students in ELD 2 have spent their childhoods in places other than the United States. They are from Mexico, El Salvador, and Peru. Most of them have been here a little over a year. The degree to which they are proficient in English varies, but generally they are all beginning English learners. Because students are placed into the class according to language ability, their ages range from 14 to 18 years old. There are 14 boys and 4 girls in the class.

The students are working on their childhood memory project—a project I hadn't taught since 1997, my first year teaching at San Lorenzo High School. Even though I was fairly confident that the project would work with this class, I hesitated for many reasons. What if the unit's success had more to do with that particular class and less to do with the curriculum itself? I recalled that we had a wonderful way of interacting with one another, and my memory was that all of the students were very willing to take risks. Other reservations stemmed from pragmatic concerns. How would I pay for the materials? Could I guarantee that the students in the science class who met in my room during third block wouldn't tamper with the paintings? And, most importantly, what valuable lessons might be forfeited while we painted for three days? Unable to reconcile these quandaries, I looked back to see if there wasn't some other unit I could do in its stead.

I noticed that many of the units I wanted to teach, such as the childhood memory project, came from my first few years teaching. I couldn't help but wonder why. Perhaps it was because as a new teacher, I gave myself more freedom and time than I do now to develop lessons that were as instructive as they were creative and engaging. I thought a lot about my students then—who they were, where they came from, what was important to them. The questions I had about my students—what they knew and what they needed to know—formed the basis of my curriculum. Planning this way was not unlike backward mapping, a current trend in curriculum development closely tied to standards-based instruction whereby a teacher identifies the standards she wants her students to have met at the unit's conclusion and then "maps backward" an instructional route to get them there.

While the process by which I plan curriculum has more or less remained the same, the climate in which I work has changed. In recent years, schools like mine have come under tremendous pressure to increase student achievement on standardized tests. The pressure is particularly acute for teachers in ELD and special education programs, whose students are required to pass tests like the California High School Exit Exam (CAHSEE) with minimal accommodations. There are moments when I think that the best thing I could do for my students would be to spend all of our time taking practice tests and completing exercises in test-prep books. I am tempted to replace the deductive teaching techniques I favor with more direct drill and practice approaches. With so much at stake, how do I justify three days of painting in an ELD class? I decided to put my fears aside and trust my instincts.

The childhood memory project requires students to complete a reflective essay, a painting, and an oral presentation based on a childhood memory. We spend the first two days of the project remembering our childhoods. We talk about the people who made us feel safe and loved. We write about the places we used to go and what we'd do when we got there. We talk about the processes of remembering, and we try to identify which of our five senses is most connected to our memories. Some students feel that their memories are most closely tied to their sense of smell; for others it is sound. If we forget something, we ask our families to help us fill in the holes. From there, we choose one person, one place, and one activity and write reflective essays focused on that person, place, and activity. From those written reflections we choose the one memory that we will paint.

As the boys prepare the room, taping newspaper to the tables, filling cups of water from the drinking fountain, stealing paper towels from the one bathroom on campus that isn't locked, several of their classmates trickle in. David and Carla admire the work of their peers before pausing in front of their own paintings, planning their next steps. Victor pokes his head in the door to make sure we are there, then runs down the hall, returning moments later with his math teacher, Mr. Cabana, in tow. Victor wants to show Mr. Cabana what he has been working on: a painting of a lake he used to go to as a child in Mazamitlan, Mexico. "When I was in love," he writes in a description of it, "here is where I liked to sit down on the little dock. This is what I did. First I sat down on the dock, then I watched the lake, and then I started to think about the girl I loved and other things like why we are

in the world, what's the mission that we have to do, and why the world
has bad things like wars."

Later, when asked, "If you could give your painting to anyone,
who would it be and why?" Victor writes, "I would give my painting
to D-1 so everybody can see what I did and remember that I was in
San Lorenzo." D-1 is Mr. Cabana's classroom and the location of the
school's study center where Victor spends quite a bit of time.

San Lorenzo serves a fairly transient population; students who begin
at San Lorenzo don't always stay there. Victor's family, for example,
plans to move to Florida in August. They've heard it's cheaper, and an
uncle who lives there has offered to help them find work and a place to
live. Despite the relatively short time Victor has attended San Lorenzo
(less than two years), he's sad to go, and he fears he'll be forgotten.

While Victor contemplates a title for his painting—he oscillates
between "The Most Beautiful Lake" and "Relax Lake"—his classmates
put the finishing touches on their projects. Some, like Victor, have
painted places they had visited with their families. Mario's painting is
of a beach near Acapulco. So is Lupe's. Others paint their schools, the
fields where they played soccer, and the parties they had to celebrate
middle school graduation. Marco paints a stunningly realistic portrait
of his first and most faithful dog, a canine with a predilection for the
legs of voluptuous women. The dog bit them with impunity until one
day the police threw Marco and his dog in prison where, Marco writes,
"We had to eat the same food, off the same plate, in the same room
for two months. We shared everything, and we could understand each
other."

On the last day of class, students present their projects. During the
first five minutes of class, students rehearse what they will say first to
themselves quietly and then orally to a partner. They are instructed to
speak in English without the aid of note cards or their essays. When the
time comes to present, each student stands beside his or her painting.
One by one, they take turns describing their paintings and the memories
that inspired them. I wish I could describe the pride they take in sharing their paintings with one another. Oral presentations in high school
classrooms can be quite nerve-racking. Self-conscious and uncertain
how to present themselves in front of a group, adolescents often dread
oral presentations as much as the teacher. But these students are anything but self-conscious. They are confident, proud, and eager to share
their accomplishments. If they can't find the word they are looking for,
one of their peers immediately comes to their aid. The audience listens

intently and asks the artist questions at the conclusion of the presentation. Class ends with a written evaluation of the course.

A few weeks after school ended, I had a chance to read through the students' course evaluations. One of the questions the students were asked was, "What was your favorite assignment?" Many students wrote about the childhood memory project. One student wrote, "I liked the memory project because it (is) good when you talk about something that you love." Mario, who had trouble completing most anything, wrote that the childhood memory project was his favorite. His reason? "I did it!" Explaining why the painting was his favorite assignment, another student responded, "because I remembered something important about my childhood."

While looking back at their paintings, rereading their papers, and sharing their responses on the course evaluation with my husband (a fellow teacher) and with some of my colleagues who know the students, I was struck by how proud they seemed to be of their work and how successful the project had been. In fact, this was one of the few projects we did that had a one hundred percent success rate. Every student completed a painting, wrote a reflective essay, and presented his or her project.

I marveled at how this came to be. I recalled that from the start, the students were engaged. From the beginning the writing happened effortlessly without any of the usual obstacles students often create for themselves to put off starting an assignment: "I don't have paper." "I don't have a pencil." "I don't know what to write." "I don't know how to start." "Can I write on something else?" "How long does it have to be?" Here was a topic they could all write about. No one had to come up with an opinion on an issue they knew little about or interpret a book that they hadn't understood or, worse, hadn't read. This assignment asked them to write about something that was important to them. In the tradition of Paolo Freire, the notable Brazilian educational theorist, the text was the students' own experience. I wonder if this project would have been as successful in a non-ELD class. ELD students are particularly poised to write about their childhood memories. Many have just undergone a major trauma in leaving their homes. Their memories are crucial to staying connected to their past and their culture. Most newcomers cannot stop thinking about their old lives and how to integrate their old lives into their new ones. Little effort is required to access these memories. Many of these students yearn to share their experiences, and this project provides them that opportunity.

Like sharing memories, painting involves risk taking. In fact, many students were more afraid of the painting requirement than the written or oral components. Part of the pleasure for me was admiring how the students overcame their initial trepidation, which they did by watching their equally inexperienced peers struggle to paint a memory. In time, those who felt they couldn't do it, did. Moreover, they loved it! They loved it because it made them feel successful. When I start worrying about the pedagogical value of spending three days painting in an English class, I remember the success the students felt and the fun we had. Isn't this one of the most important aims of educators: to build students' personal portfolios of successful learning so that later on, when students are about to face a challenge, they can point to a time when they took a risk, met the challenge, and succeeded?

Other legitimate educational goals are served by this lesson—goals I developed through conversations I had with colleagues in planning this lesson and establishing the structures that would need to be in place to ensure its success. This is common at my school. We often look to one another to create student support structures that are based on our perceptions of our students' needs. While it is abundantly obvious that our students need to learn to perform better on standardized tests, they also need to learn the myriad skills addressed by this unit. For example, the unit requires them to apply linguistic skills and the narrative and descriptive techniques necessary in autobiographical writing. They build oral language skills and practice the art of public speaking. They learn to recall memories and to sort and select the most vivid one from all their memories. They learn how to capture memory in words and how to seek the help of others for details. They learn how to memorialize their images in painting—and that painting, as with their writing, requires sorting and selecting, making choices about content, detail, color, emphasis, and context. Perhaps most importantly, as with Victor, the young man who wanted to leave his work with D-1, they learn that their creations leave a legacy and their memorials are valuable and valued.

And yet, I continue to wonder how relevant all this is to preparing my students for the CAHSEE, and how capable I am of preparing English learners to pass a standardized test in English, without the aid of a dictionary or directions in Spanish. Several years ago, students taking the CAHSEE were asked to read a passage about hummingbirds and then to write about them. I wonder how many of my ELD students have ever heard the word "hummingbird" in English, much less seen it written. Although many of my students demonstrated marked improvement in writing by the end of the year, they still have a long way to go. Learning a language takes time, a willingness to make mistakes, trust, support, and lots of practice. Seeing how far they've come and knowing how far they still need to go makes me wonder whether it's even fair to ask, for example, a 16-year-old who has only just begun to learn English to take a comprehensive test like the CAHSEE. The vocabulary is so specific, and the student's level of understanding is so limited.

Regardless of all of my doubts, I still feel like this project represents my teaching and my students at our best. They were engaged and successful, and Mario's proclamation, "I liked it because I did it!" is not just a statement of completion, but an exuberant declaration of the pride that comes from accomplishing complex, challenging tasks and doing them well. Is this not, at least in some measure, academic success?

❖ ❖ ❖

Commentary

JUDY BEBELAAR

Although teenagers are perhaps not as tough a crowd as an Elizabethan audience at the Globe, they are not always easy to hook. Shakespeare knew he had to engage his audience right from the start, using thunder, lightning, and the evil incantations of three witches in *Macbeth*; the urgent cacophony of storm and shipwreck in *The Tempest*; and a parade of gorgeously attired Athenians and the announcement of a marriage between the Duke and the Queen of the Amazons in *A Midsummer Night's Dream*. High school teachers face a similar imperative; if a lesson doesn't initially pull students in so that they are ready to meet a challenge, meaningful learning probably won't take place. A demanding lesson must have a good act one, scene one. Once the stage is set, the drama can unfold, leading to the hard work that reading with a purpose, thinking critically, and writing clearly and cogently requires.

Dorothy Russo's childhood memory project lesson has that pull. Like all good teachers, Russo knows her students well. Realizing that many beginning English learners have just undergone "a major trauma in leaving their homes," she decides to use a project that will allow them to begin to integrate memories of their former lives into their new experiences by sharing remembrances of a loved person or place.

Russo knows her students would want to make their very best effort at writing, painting, and speaking; they owe it to the beloved memory. And they would have an audience for this piece of the past brought to life—not their teacher alone, but their fellow-traveler classmates as well. Russo doesn't give us the whole story of the lesson from its original form in 1997, when she was a new teacher at the school. However, I am sure that like many of my own favorite lessons, hers changed and improved over the years that she developed as a teacher and learned from her students—just as a play develops after many performances.

Russo follows her instincts and gives this project to her students rather than spending all of their time "taking practice tests and completing exercises in test-prep books." Her faith and courage should serve as a model to others in this time of test score anxiety for schools and teachers. The best teaching practices result both in skills developed *and* in habits of learning that students can take with them.

The childhood memory project has several ingredients crucial to success:

- Students have *ample time*—time for thinking to emerge, time to think through their memories and talk about them, and time to make revisions and adjustments.
- Students have *multiple avenues for success*. There's a good chance that students will feel some comfort with at least one of the required modes of expression: speaking, painting, and writing.
- Because the project has an end product, this lesson helps students add to *a portfolio of positive achievements* while encouraging them *to take the risks* necessary for learning and growing. Project-oriented learning gives students a concrete chunk of learning, something to look at, remember, and use as a model.
- The project builds a *supportive community of learners*.
- Students learn the value of thoughtful *preparation, reflection, and revision.*

Russo gives the lesson time and space so students feel a sense of continuity. She helps them prepare for the final performance. She begins with two days of talking about memories. Sharing this kind of personal experience starts to build a community in the classroom. And Russo wisely guides the memory talk so that her students aren't silenced by the feeling they have nothing worthy to contribute or get sidetracked into the kind of gossip teenagers enjoy; she asks them to talk about "the people that made us feel safe and loved," "the places we used to go and what we'd do when we got there," and "which of our five senses is most connected to our memories." She encourages consultation with others as students ask their "families to help fill in the holes." The memories of others undoubtedly spark more of a student's own recollections. Thus, she helps students gather writing material, organize it, and supplement it.

Russo's class is small by most public school standards, only 18 students. In a larger class, a teacher might want to have students make written lists first, then move into small groups before sharing with the entire class, so that everyone would have a chance to share, build confidence, and get help with English words before speaking to the whole class.

She allows time for writing the three reflective essays, presumably with feedback from the teacher and time for revision at home, and she gives students time to choose their best or most meaningful piece. I imagine that some of the best were read to the class as a whole, or perhaps students shared in small groups. Good student models are often the best inspiration for beginning writers. I wonder if Victor's essay hung next to his painting in D-1 for all students to see and appreciate. I hope so.

There are the three days of painting, which probably involve more talking and reflection as well as feedback from others. And there is time to rehearse for the final presentation, both alone and with a small group as an audience. Prompting, in the form of peer support, is encouraged: "If they can't find the word they are looking for, one of their peers immediately comes to their aid."

The fact that the final act for the course is a reflection on the year, and that many of the students chose the childhood memory project as their favorite reinforces the theme I see in Russo's description of the piece, and I imagine I would see in some form in all of her lessons: reflection.

Russo takes her students from autobiographical writing, one of the forms with which beginning writers can find success, to an introductory experience with one of the most sophisticated types, the reflective essay. When my colleagues at an inner-city school in San Francisco and I planned our first schoolwide writing sample, we were looking for a type that would be applicable across the curriculum and useful in preparation for college writing. We reviewed the eight types

of writing—autobiographical incident, controversial issue, evaluation, interpretation, observational writing, reflective essay, report of
information, speculation about causes and effects—described in the
California Assessment Program Writing Guide issued by the California
Department of Education. We chose the reflective essay.

The booklet provides the following description of a reflective essay:

> The writing of a successful reflective essay requires the ability to see
> connections. Moving from a personal experience or a general concept,
> the writer must explore possibilities, try out ideas, and reach beyond
> personal implications to a larger, more general significance. Seeing con-
> nections is a central component of problem solving, one of the critical
> aspects of thinking. (The reflective essay) asks for understandings that
> delve into and explore what we have in common—the universal truth of
> what it means to be human beings.

Although Russo wisely does not have this beginning-level English
language development class write an essay that must arrive at a general
concept and a larger significance, the students must have seen connections among themselves through the presentations of their paintings,
and others must have had more than a glimpse of "what we have in
common." And Victor's essay, "When I Was in Love," expresses well
some of the universal human truths: "This is what I did. First I sat
down on the dock, then I watched the lake and then I started to think
about the girl I loved and other things like: why we are in the world,
what's the mission that we have to do, and why the world has bad
things like wars." Russo's students may not have written a reflective
essay as described in the above definition, but they are certainly poised,
when their vocabularies and writing skills are more developed, to write
a deeper essay about the experience of leaving their homelands. And
they have begun to see the power of emotional memory, realizing that
writing that comes from deeply felt passages of personal history can
speak to a reader and as with a play, can help an actor connect with
an audience.

The lesson has many transferable skills. As Russo points out, students have to sort and select among ideas, topics, and pieces of writing.
They learn valuable presentation techniques. They make connections
between themselves and their classmates. Together, they "put on a
show."

At first Russo feels guilty, but her instinct to revive her old lesson and
help her students tell their stories is right. It is Russo's engaging act one,
scene one, that hooks her students; gives the project its one hundred

percent success rate; and causes Julio, Jorge, and Pablo, who usually are late to class, to arrive 30 minutes early, at 7:30 a.m., to be sure they are prepared for the final presentation. She "hooks" her students at the beginning, but then she moves them to the greater challenges of reflection. She pulls them into wanting to do the hard work that good writing requires, and she has prepared students to move from autobiographical incident to thinking and writing about universal significance.

Shakespeare in *Romeo and Juliet* begins the play with a sonnet spoken by the chorus. Then he has Romeo and Juliet, when they first meet, speak a sonnet together (the beautiful vocal pas de deux that begins with Romeo saying, "If I profane with my unworthiest hand/ This holy shrine . . ." in Act I, Scene V). He ends the play with Capulet and Montague speaking what comes very close to being a sonnet, with the Prince adding the final couplet, "For never was a story of more woe/Than this of Juliet and her Romeo." Dorothy Russo's lesson resonates with memory, shared emotion, and experience, but then it moves students from simply feeling like a community sharing memories to creating a kind of collective drama, complete with the backdrop of their paintings, recurring themes, and an affirmation of their lives.

❖ ❖ ❖

Commentary

ALICE KAWAZOE

We've all seen those commercials on television touting the virtues of some medicine and concluding with warnings of possible adverse side effects: "Evacuix is guaranteed to clear sinuses completely, but prolonged use may result in insomnia, gangrene, gingivitis, or sexual dysfunction." Beginning teachers should be given the warning: "Teaching will be satisfying and challenging, but prolonged participation may result in psychosis." Dorothy Russo's case study is an apt example of a kind of educational psychosis.

In education we relish dichotomies and shun the direct, straightforward response. We consider issues in terms of oppositional forces or worse, reduce complex discussions to a series of either/ors. Whole language vs. phonics, independent vs. small group learning, small learning communities vs. large comprehensive schools, block scheduling vs. traditional scheduling, left brain vs. right brain, cognitive vs. affective, English learners vs. native speakers, private vs. public schools, vouchers vs. no vouchers, administration vs. teachers, and on and on.

But as Wilma Taggart, a fine veteran teacher once said, "What's interesting is not one side or the other; what's interesting is the 'versus.'" In other words, how do schools and teachers make sense of it all and keep from swinging, like some giant scythe, from one extreme to another? How do they find the middle ground where the learners' reality resides?

Dorothy Russo is caught in a now too-familiar either/or quandary. Torn between preparing students for standardized tests and engaging students in a writing, speaking, and artistic learning experience, she asks, ". . . what valuable lessons might be forfeited while we paint for three days?" She has developed a complex, challenging, multi-faceted unit, focused on developing the oral and writing skills of her English learners and giving them the rare opportunity to capture an image from their childhood in a painting. And yet, she feels guilty usurping time from test preparation to teach, of all things, writing and linguistic skills.

What kind of crazed place has school become when a talented teacher like Dorothy, committed to her students struggling to learn English, concedes, "There are moments when I think that the best thing I could do for my students would be to spend all of our time taking practice tests and completing exercises in test-prep books."

Her better self tells Dorothy that her students deserve more. She suffers from the sin of caring for her students, "who they were, where they came from, what was important to them," and importantly, she cares about their learning "what they knew and what they needed to know."

I'm reminded of the words of Huck Finn, who turns against society and follows his conscience when he chooses to escape with Jim, the runaway slave: "All right, then, I'll go to hell!" Dorothy isn't going to hell, but she suffers with doubt when she decides "to put [her] fears aside and trust [her] instincts," and her guilt persists even after her students produce their best writing and unforgettable artwork. I wish she included more of her students' writing in this case study so we could read their narratives and see their improvement.

Dorothy, and other conscientious teachers like her, need to be reminded of the middle ground. Yes, her students would benefit from taking practice tests and some test preparation. But a course devoted wholly to test preparation would relegate her students to the lowest level of learning, dreary remedial learning—if not learners' hell, at best, learners' limbo.

Dorothy's greater responsibility is to develop the reading, writing, speaking, and language skills of her English learners, and her complex, multi-layered unit does just that. The unit addresses three major California English-language arts content standards:

· Write biographical or autobiographical narratives.

· Write and speak with a command of standard English conventions.

· Deliver narrative presentations.

The unit demands high levels of thinking, writing, and speaking applications: focusing on a topic, using sensory details, sequencing, and reflecting on significance. And further, the unit helps prepare students for the writing section of the state tests.

We have to free conscientious teachers like Dorothy Russo from the pressure to slavishly adhere to test preparation materials and relieve them of the guilt they feel when they stray from the materials' narrow dictates. Effective test preparation must be transformed into effective instruction and serve broader goals than higher scores on standardized tests. Improved scores are important, but more important are student achievement in the classroom and student learning assessed weekly, not annually.

A critical question we have yet to answer fully is: how do emergent English learners in high school best learn in a few years? We know students in elementary grades can learn English with surprising speed. But we are less successful with teenagers, newly exposed to English and sometimes not literate in their native language.

We know improved learning in the classroom will, in time, be reflected in higher scores for English learners. However, the various publics are not very patient. We must continually remind ourselves that accountability means we are accountable, not just to the federal and state governments, not just to the community and its realtors. But we are accountable to our students, and their learning—measured over the span of days, weeks, months, and years—is the most meaningful register of our efforts. Using that measure, Dorothy Russo's API (Academic Performance Index) is off the charts.

The Collaborative for Higher Education High School Mathematics/Science Enrichment Project

*Reflections from the Director
and Two Teachers*

EDWARD LANDESMAN
ADAM RANDALL
LEO FLORENDO

ED LANDESMAN CONCEIVED of this dynamic partnership of high schools, higher education, NASA/Ames, and industry to interest and involve more underrepresented students in science, math, and engineering careers. He describes the collaborative's complex components and the challenges of implementing and sustaining the project. Two masterful teachers, Adam Randall and Leo Florendo, discuss the details, difficulties, and rewards of seeing students achieve in science and math as never before.

❖ ❖ ❖

A DIRECTOR'S PERSPECTIVE OF THE PROJECT—
ED LANDESMAN

Project Overview

To attract more qualified underrepresented youth into careers in engineering and science, the Collaborative for Higher Education (De Anza College; Foothill College; San Jose State University; and the University of California, Santa Cruz), together with NASA/Ames and with support from CAPP, began working with two high schools (Los Altos High School in the Mountain View/Los Altos Union High School District and Homestead High School in the Fremont Union High School District) on a three-year project that would feature curriculum enrichment in mathematics and physics, a summer science camp, summer internships, a high school engineering course, and visits to local science and technology complexes, and local colleges. I am a University of California, Santa Cruz (UCSC) Professor Emeritus of Mathematics and currently the Education Director of the Collaborative for Higher Education; I serve as director for this project.

Instructors from De Anza and Foothill Colleges teamed with teachers from the two high schools to provide curriculum enrichment for a targeted group of eleventh-grade students who would enroll in second-year algebra and physics as a cohort. The college instructors worked with the teachers to identify important links between mathematics and physics so that students would see the connections as they learned each subject. The curriculum enrichment was supplemented with some of the hands-on applied scientific educational modules already developed by NASA/Ames. Students had the opportunity to visit the NASA/Ames site during the school year and use these scientific modules. The modules' content was linked to students' current courses and provided pertinent applications not normally encountered in the classroom. Trips to the San Francisco Exploratorium, Hiller Space Museum, NASA/Ames Wind Tunnel, the Search for Extraterrestrial Intelligence Institute (SETI), Minolta Planetarium at De Anza College, and San Jose Tech Museum provided additional motivation.

During the summer following the eleventh-grade enrichment, the students attended a two-week science camp taught by some of the same high school instructors. The students then took on four-week, half-time internships at NASA/Ames or in local industry. At the camp, the students worked on applied scientific projects, including building electronic equipment such as radio receivers and transmitters, constructing websites, building stick bridges that supported two hundred times their weight, and constructing and programming some elementary robots. This practical experience prepared the students for their internships, which allowed them to work with researchers in science, engineering, and technology. Students received stipends and high school science credit for their summer activities. In the twelfth grade, students took an introductory college course in engineering. The course, taught by an instructor from the Foothill/De Anza Community College District, provided students with an understanding of the different subfields within engineering and the challenges and academic requirements for each. Before applying to college, the students visited UC Santa Cruz, San Jose

State University, and De Anza College. These collaborative and varied approaches inspired many of these students to pursue scientific studies in college and to subsequently choose careers in these disciplines.

In its second year, the project has expanded to include two high schools, James Lick High School and Yerba Buena High School, in the East Side Union High School District. Each of these schools has a very high population of underrepresented students who are being brought into the science, technology, engineering, and mathematics (STEM) pipeline.

Partnerships

This CAPP project, as is the case with most other CAPP projects, has three major institutional partners: higher education, industry, and schools.

Higher Education: From higher education, one or more professors or instructors in education, science, mathematics, or engineering often form the core team. From industry, one or more individuals from the human resources division or other departments that want to help support the upcoming generation of potential employees may be the participants. And from the schools, the participants are most often teachers who are looking for innovative ways to teach science and mathematics and to motivate students who often are not performing to full capability.

Industry: The industry partner is NASA/Ames. The applications of mathematics and physics at the NASA/Ames base and the desire to attract the next generation of students to undertake the challenges the nation faces in science, technology, engineering, and mathematics, as well as the importance of attracting students from underrepresented populations, positioned NASA/Ames most favorably. The additional advantage of having NASA/Ames physically located in close proximity to the targeted schools made it an ideal choice.

Working with NASA/Ames led to some unforeseen educational benefits for all CAPP partners. The project team recognized early the benefit of students visiting the Aeronautics Education Laboratory at NASA/Ames. This large facility had numerous modules for students to simulate air traffic control, use a flight simulator, and design airfoils, using computer-assisted technology. The applications were not only instructive, but provided real-life applications of the algebra and physics that students were learning in their classes. When the teachers and I visited the facility and previewed the modules, the teachers recognized the value of the modules, but each saw ways to enhance the modules' handouts. I requested permission from the lab administrator to allow the teachers to modify these handouts. The teacher team had clearly exhibited the expertise to gain the confidence of the NASA personnel, so we received permission. The teachers made excellent modifications that optimized student learning. Subsequently, these revised materials were incorporated into the modules and were distributed at the facility. Because both the NASA personnel and the teachers were open to improving the materials, the partners collaboratively strengthened the modules.

Another benefit from the partnership took place over two summers. The teachers in the project and I helped the NASA/Ames Educational Technology team in their work on two projects. One project involved the development of learning materials for flight takeoff and landing. Another project developed learning materials for a personal satellite assistant robot that may assist future shuttle astronauts and the space station. For the latter project, NASA presented the team with a group achievement award.

Schools: Initially, we chose two high schools whose student achievement, as a whole, was quite respectable. However, each had a segment of its population that was not achieving at the same levels as the majority. It was that segment that we targeted to be our initial cohort. After many discussions with the administrators at the Mountain View/Los Altos Union High School District, I began conversations with teachers Adam Randall and Leo Florendo, physics and mathematics teachers at Los Altos High School (LAHS). Both men had excellent backgrounds in mathematics and physics and had a history of successfully working together. Their previous successes had typically been with high-achieving students and students interested in robotics. Working with a more challenging student population represented a new career phase for these teachers, and they were willing to take on that challenge.

At Homestead High, after discussion with the chairs of mathematics and physics departments, I chose a physics teacher new to the district and a veteran mathematics teacher. Later, when the project was extended to the East Side Union High School District in San Jose, I worked with both seasoned and energetic young mathematics instructors and physics and chemistry teachers. These teachers were truly dedicated to achieving success with our targeted student population that represented most of the students at the schools.

In addition to working with the teachers, it is extremely important to make connections with the administration, particularly, principals and district associate superintendents in charge of curriculum. Administrators support their teachers' work and model the importance of that work by attending the meetings related to the project, providing necessary resources, and rewarding the teachers for their participation and for positive student outcomes. Drawing in administrators entails continually updating them on the challenges and achievements. Each principal and district administrator involved with this project has been supportive and an advocate for the work.

The challenge was to create a partnership where higher education, industry, and the schools would share commitment and responsibility, and all the participants would work together and support each other to meet the project's goals. The dedication from participants far exceeded the everyday work experience.

Two Teachers

When I have worked on projects in the schools, I have always attributed any success to the participating teachers and administrators. The teachers see the students each day, motivate the students, and are the role models for the students. When I was asked to write about this CAPP project, I immediately assigned a good portion of the task to two of the highly successful teachers, Adam Randall and Leo Florendo. Their accounts of their experiences follow.

A TEACHER'S PERSPECTIVE OF THE PROJECT— ADAM RANDALL

Several systems need to be in place to successfully pull off something like the Collaborative for Higher Education's High School Mathematics/ Science Enrichment Project, including leadership, vision, commitment, resources, creativity, and students willing to take responsibility for their own education and future.

When Ed Landesman first approached Leo Florendo and me to recruit students who were "underrepresented" in the University of California and California State University systems, who often did not take science or math classes beyond the minimum requirements to graduate from high school, and who rarely went into science, technology, engineering, or mathematics-related careers and then to enroll them in "enhanced" high level math and science classes, and motivate them to become college bound and major in STEM fields and ultimately STEM careers . . . I was in a state of shock! I thought to myself, "Who is this guy and what did he have for breakfast? Of course, I'm interested. That's why I became a physics teacher! I want all of my students to major in STEM, develop amazing skills, and become captains of industry."

However, after teaching in a public high school for several years, my initial enthusiasm to change every student into a physicist waned. I quickly realized that most students did not care about mathematics and its intrinsic beauty. Most students did not even realize how special their own lives were, much less life in general or the properties of their universe. Most students did not see the usefulness of the interconnectedness of mathematics and science, and the ability to model nature and gain predictive power within it. Most students were simply going through the motions, trying to please me, the teacher, to get the highest grade for doing the minimum amount of work.

As Ed continued to share his vision of the project and the commitment and resources given to the program, I was overwhelmed. The feeling of support, understanding, shared vision, and leadership was inspiring. This was not someone's half-baked idea to improve standardized test scores of some of California's lowest achieving students. This was a well-planned, detail-oriented, highly connected project to give underrepresented students a real chance at positively changing their lives by earning a meaningful education.

As excited as Leo and I were to share Ed's vision, reality and our natural skepticism set in. The students we were trying to reach were 16 and 17 years old. They had not developed the academic, logic, or study skills necessary to succeed in college preparatory STEM courses. They had become hardened and skeptical and were trained to believe that they were not smart and not good at math and science. They regarded adults and teachers who professed, "Education is the key to success" or "If you focus your mind, you can become anything your heart desires," as lame and out of touch with reality.

Truthfully, it is hard enough to teach motivated, academically oriented high school students to become skilled practitioners of mathematics and physics. How were we going to turn this other group around, especially in only two class periods? The reality is that all the vision, leadership, commitment, resources, and creativity in the world were not going to turn these kids around . . . unless they wanted to make the turn themselves.

If we were right about needing just the right students who were ready and willing to make a change, then one of the most important tasks was the student recruitment process. We not only had to identify which students were demographically "underrepresented" in the STEM university environment, but which of them had an underlying, natural intellectual curiosity. We had to, in a sense, become academic detectives.

At the time Leo and I were looking to recruit students, we were also teaching full-time, involved with other school-related activities, and trying to maintain healthy family and social lives as well. We didn't have direct access to or training in using the school's student database. We did not know how to even generate a list of viable students.

Almost before we could ask for it, Brigitte Sarraf, the district's Associate Superintendent for Educational Services, rescued us. She provided a list of students who fit the "underrepresented" criteria. She has been an amazing advocate of the program and has streamlined processes, smoothed political bumps, and given continual, unwavering support.

Once we had the list of students, we shared it with each student's previous math and science teachers. We looked for anecdotal evidence of students' underperformance due to lack of skills, not bad attitudes. We heard stories of how students underperformed, but they had natural intellectual curiosity and were not afraid to work hard. Teachers would look through the list and point out students who seemed to need just a little more time to grasp the material and who might benefit from a nontraditional high school STEM class. Eventually, we identified a core group of students who we thought fit the "underrepresented" criteria and had the intellectual curiosity and ability to learn STEM material well beyond their current academic placement.

Next, we had to see if these students were even interested in taking part in such an academically rigorous, potentially life-changing experience and in making such a long-term commitment. How do you get over 50 teenagers to take time out of their busy lives to come and hear how they should stop being satisfied with underperforming academically and start working harder than they have ever worked before? We ordered pizza, lots of pizza, and invited them to lunch!

Leo and I asked Ed to arrange for scientists and engineers from

NASA/Ames in Mountain View to attend the lunch and give a short presentation about what they do. Of equal importance, we wanted the scientists and engineers to look like the students. We wanted to make sure the students would not be looking at middle-aged white men with masking tape holding their glasses together, but instead would be looking at people with the same color skin, or same native language or gender. We wanted the students to be able to visualize themselves in the roles of the presenters. The NASA/Ames presenters hit a home run. There were female astrobiologists and Hispanic and Middle Eastern engineers and astronomers; there was even a helicopter test pilot. The presentation was short, and the NASA/Ames presenters sat down with the students and had face-to-face conversations. The luncheon was a success and inspired many of the students to sign up. However, many of the students who were invited did not even bother to come.

Besides the difficulties of recruiting students, the creation and implementation of a new academic program during a time of school and district-wide budget cuts and financial uncertainties was stressful and nerve-racking. Not only did it bring an enormous amount of attention to our classrooms from administrators and other teachers, it also put Leo and me up against other teachers who were working to save their unique academic programs from the district's budgetary chopping block.

Existing academic programs that had long been thought of as part of the school culture were undergoing serious budgetary review. As a result, many academic programs were going to be significantly reduced or completely cut from district funding. In contrast, receiving resources for something brand new made the pre-engineering program, and Leo and me, targets for schoolwide gossip. How could we possibly be asking to expand the academic offerings with a series of new classes while fellow teachers were being laid off and other seemingly worthwhile, long-term programs were being cut?

Teacher to teacher, it was hard to find anyone who disagreed with what the pre-engineering program was designed to do. Who could disagree with giving such an enormous opportunity to the student demographic that we were trying to reach? Of course, it was a good idea, but how was it going to be paid for? The answer began by describing CAPP's role in the program. The CAPP grant would fund significant components of the program.

Another huge issue was deciding what "enhancing the curriculum" meant. Instructional minutes were already spread thin teaching to the state standards. Yet we knew that to "hook" this group of students, we needed to break away from much of the traditional pedagogy and build fundamental layers of excitement and relevance to the students' daily lives. Enhancing the curriculum ended up coming in two specific forms: internal classroom teaching enhancement and external experiential enhancement. Internally, Leo and I worked to match concepts and skills in algebra with those in physics. The result was a combined reinforcement of algebra in physics and physics in algebra.

For example, when the students were studying algebraic substitutions, factoring, graphing, or linear systems in algebra, they would use the skills to solve physics problems. Often simply using the same vocabulary in physics that they used in algebra helped students connect the two seemingly separate disciplines.

Another method we used was to incorporate as much technology as possible. Students, working in pairs, learned to create spreadsheets to record, then analyze experimental data and compare them to the mathematical models we created describing the event. We used probeware to gather enormous quantities of experimental data and then imported the data in spreadsheets for further analysis. The probeware changed the focus of the lab time from gathering and recording data to analyzing and interpreting the data. As a result, we had more time to think about the physics in question and its mathematical description.

We also used video cameras and digital projectors to enhance demonstrations. We videotaped two dimensional projectiles launched with specific initial conditions and then used video editing software to slow the event down and watch it frame by frame, sometimes overlaying vector quantities to help with student learning. We used clips from popular movies to demonstrate Newton's laws of motion, gravitation, circular motion, or the impulse-momentum theorem. Hollywood sometimes gets the physics right, and sometimes it does not. We would show examples of both and try to get students to figure out which was which.

External classroom enhancement came in the form of field trips to technology and science centers, paid summer science day camp, and paid internships. We were concerned that the field trips would not only take away from instructional time in our classes, but also disrupt the students' other classes. To minimize the disruption, our school administrators scheduled the project's physics and algebra classes during fifth and sixth periods. As a result, we could leave on a field trip at the beginning of lunch and return before the school day ended. The students only missed either physics or algebra or both classes and could be back in time to participate in school athletic programs or other activities.

As for field trips, we always planned two trips to the San Francisco Exploratorium, one in the beginning of the year, and one toward the end. The idea was to stimulate the students' minds with dozens of really cool demonstrations that manipulated combinations of physical and physiological phenomena and initiated the response in students, "How does that work?" We could then draw on the experience at the Exploratorium throughout the rest of the school year as we taught much of the material that would help students understand what they saw and questioned. Our last field trip was back to the Exploratorium. This time students were armed with a lot more conceptual understanding. As a result, they were able to explain the basics of what they were observing and ask even more questions and identify even more that they did not understand.

One time, on our first trip to the Exploratorium, a student really liked an optical experiment, which used a series of plane and concave mirrors to create the illusion of a large iron bolt being suspended in mid-air. The illusion was so good that she could reach for the bolt fully believing that she could grasp it and remove it, only to have her hand pass right through what was really the bolt's image. The student spent a lot of time interacting with the illusion and returned to it several times during our first trip. Later in the school year when we studied geometric optics and the formation of real and virtual images by mirror reflections, she brought up this illusion. I was able to use that as a "hook" to get students to pay attention to the ray diagrams used to predict image formation.

When we returned to the Exploratorium near the end of the year, I noticed the same student walking immediately to the optical illusion demonstration. She was much more interested in following the ray diagram and text explanation posted next to the illusion. She was more curious about the actual shape of the mirrors used and even attempted to stick her head inside the viewing hole to see what was really going on. She carefully viewed the illusion from as many different angles as she could with different combinations of fingers interacting with the image. The illusion demonstration had been enhanced since our first trip. Someone had attached a small penlight on a string and encouraged viewers to shine light through the view hole on the iron bolt. Amazingly, the suspended bolt became illuminated, only adding to the effect that the bolt was really suspended in space. The student and I smiled with excitement and awe. I listened to her talk about the ray diagram. It was obvious that she had understood a significant amount of the optical concepts and vocabulary that we had learned in class, but she still could not really get her mind around this amazing and advanced demonstration. In some sense, a good measure that a student has learned something meaningful is hearing them admit, by asking deeper probing questions, that they do not really understand it at all.

On another field trip we went to the offices of SETI in Mountain View. Dr. Frank Drake, a member of the National Academy of Sciences, a world-class astronomer, and the creator of the famous Drake Equation, which predicts the probability of finding extraterrestrial life, was to give a presentation to the pre-engineering students. Before the field trip Leo and I engaged the students in a conversation about the existence of life in the universe other than on Earth, and we did our best to explain the Drake Equation to them.

Their interest level was very high, and they were in awe to meet Dr. Drake and hear him speak. It was an amazing educational experience for the students, many of whom had never seriously considered the existence of extraterrestrial life or the methods scientists used to search for it. By the end of the field trip, students were standing in line to get Dr. Drake's autograph. Students were once again looking into the application of STEM far beyond anything they had ever imagined.

Another positive side effect from the collaboration was a chance for Leo and me to work with NASA/Ames, Nick Fiori (Foothill College math instructor), and Hassan Bourgoub (De Anza College math instructor) on redesigning learning modules for the Aeronautics Experience Laboratory (AEL). We worked with NASA scientists supervising the summer internships and with NASA's education office designing and testing a physics curriculum.

Ed Landesman's ability to bring so many disparate physical and personnel resources together is amazing. As teachers in this project, Leo and I have the ability to be as creative as possible, to dream up the wildest ideas to motivate and excite the kids, and Ed will consider them and most often turn them into a reality.

Leo and I once suggested that taking the students to NASA/Ames' Moffett Field campus would be interesting, but taking them for a ride in a helicopter once they got there would really spark their interest. We truly believed a helicopter ride would have been really great, but there would be no way Ed would go for it. It was almost a test to see how far he would go for the students. Leo and I learned our lesson. Ed seriously tried to get the helicopter ride, but he was denied by almost every agency involved primarily for safety and legal reasons. What he did negotiate was a private tour of a research helicopter hangar where students could see, firsthand, helicopters being fitted with electronics and instrumentation that totally sparked their interest.

Ed's level of commitment to the Collaborative's vision, his attention to detail, and his ability to motivate those he works with to achieve excellence is the driving force that has positioned the mathematic/ science enrichment project to become a permanent pathway to success at Los Altos High School. Sure, Leo and I are on the front lines working directly with the students, but without Ed's frequent updates, clear communication, leadership, long-term planning, and vision, the project would not be anywhere near the quality program it has become.

ANOTHER TEACHER'S PERSPECTIVE OF THE PROJECT—
LEO FLORENDO

In virtually every successful organization, success largely depends on a clear and worthwhile vision and purpose. The STEM program has such a vision: "To encourage and support more underrepresented students to pursue and to be successful in higher level math, science, and technology courses in high school and college. Ultimately, our hope is to see our students be successful in a career in a STEM field." The program enjoys support from all levels—CAPP, school district officials, school administrators, other teachers at the school, and students, along with their families. I can not imagine anyone saying, "What a worthless program! It's doing the wrong thing for kids." The STEM program, with its vision, does do the right thing for students.

Students chosen for the STEM program are typically undecided about everything, apathetic toward learning, and not necessarily exposed to the concept of how education, especially math and science, can be useful in life. After explaining the program's vision to these students, they have more buy-in to learning because their learning reaches beyond the 50 minutes a day of mathematics or science. Students who do not normally see the value of learning in school begin to see the value of a focused and meaningful education because of the overarching STEM program vision that will lead them for several years in high school, through college, and into their careers.

Of course, there are many challenges to make any vision, no matter how worthy or noble, truly work. I will address those later, but the vision of the program and the commitment of time and effort make those challenges less burdensome and more rewarding for all involved.

Without people to make the vision a reality, the vision is words on paper in some binder on a shelf. In the past seven years, Los Altos High School has had six principals and two WASC committee visitations. I have come to realize that good leadership gives vision clarity and momentum. A leader or leaders have to not only start the fire, but keep the fire burning strong. I am just a teacher, and I take the responsibility for teaching students in front of me. This kind of program requires someone outside the classroom to complete tasks that I do not have the time to do and honestly do not know how to do. For our STEM program, Ed Landesman is that person. I do not know anyone else who not only has the contacts in so many organizations in education and industry, but also has the knowledge, experience, savvy, courage, and respect to convince all of those contacts to support this program. I was truly awed by the credentials of all the 50 or so program partners who were brought together by Ed. As much as I tell my students about the amount of support that makes their program work, it is not as impressive as actually seeing the 50 people in one room. I wish I could recreate that scene of supporters every year for my students to see and have it sink into their minds just how important they are to so many people.

When I describe to my students and their families the unique two years they will experience in our program and the option to attend Foothill College through the Developing Effective Engineering Pathways (DEEP) program, which potentially guarantees admittance into the University of California, Santa Cruz School of Engineering after two years, suddenly their previously vague academic and career plans for the next six years become much clearer. Perhaps more importantly, because of this pipeline to the future, a career in STEM becomes much more believable to students. This pipeline gives me a very convincing argument to change the mindset of both students and families. I have seen so many students who, once they have a vision of their goals, begin to transform themselves into powerful and amazing students.

Many times we have heard, "Teachers should be respected and paid more." Personally, I truly appreciate the respect and fair compensation that reward me for the extra energy and bold choices I put into making this program work. When I tell my colleagues about our program and the opportunities and rewards it brings, many of them beg to be part of it. If this kind of program is to be established elsewhere, I would hope that managers afford the teachers the respect, compensation, material support, and freedom to make bold choices as Ed has done for us. Above all, Ed clearly does all of this because he truly cares about these students.

Adam and I work hard to become better teachers, and we constantly tweak what we do to improve our teaching. Importantly, we are physics majors primarily teaching physics at LAHS, unlike at many other high schools where biology or chemistry majors may teach physics, partly because physics majors do not often become teachers. Both of us truly enjoy teaching physics because we get to play with concepts and the "toys" and "gadgets" used to help students learn these concepts. We believe so much of physics can be made tangible to students, unlike balancing equations in chemistry or learning weather patterns in earth science. Students can readily recognize physics every day and everywhere. We try our best to have them look at the world through a physics lens while they are driving, playing volleyball, burning a CD, or putting up holiday lights. Because we ourselves are such physics "geeks" and proud of it, teaching physics comes naturally to us. We immerse ourselves in the subject. Every successful class I have experienced always included a qualified teacher who knew the subject intimately and who could apply the subject to the real world. To replicate the STEM program requires the right people for the right positions and for the right reasons.

I teach Algebra II from a physics perspective. We really try to make the connections clear between Algebra II and physics by making the algebra problems similar to the physics problems. In some cases, the line between algebra and physics is blurred because we design the lessons that way. Both of us are competent in both physics and math. We plan to switch classes at given times this coming year; I will suddenly teach physics during the allocated algebra period, and Adam will teach algebra in the allocated physics period, just to make the connections between math and physics even stronger. When possible in algebra, I will use familiar topics from physics.

Adam and I are both technically savvy with computers, robotics, mechanics, electricity, and gadgets, and we incorporate many of these items into our lessons. Students learn in many different ways, and manipulatives, especially technical items, typically excite students. Our students use computers, motion sensors, spreadsheets, various graphing and regression functions on calculators, robot programming techniques, projectiles, multi-meters, and other equipment to solidify their understanding of concepts and to make connections between physics and math.

Adam and I frequently communicate and collaborate. Often we will bounce teaching ideas off of each other. We willingly share ideas. We laugh at our little failures. We tweak what needs modification. Materials are sometimes hard to find, but we willingly share everything. I know collaboration happens at other schools too, but what makes our situation unique is that the communication between us is natural and not forced. Our STEM program would not be as successful without the personal and professional relationship between us, a relationship that may not be measurable, but is essential to the program.

If a similar program is to be initiated elsewhere, a "natural," rather than a "forced" team, is crucial. I recall meeting with two teachers at another school who were asked to start the STEM program. Almost immediately I knew the program would not even get off the ground because of the lack of chemistry between the two teachers.

The students chosen for the STEM program are neither academic stars nor failures; they are from the middle group of students who may need a little something extra to get them over that "hump" in "getting" math and science. If we want different results from these students, we need to try something different in the way we teach them.

Here's a refreshing thought: pay students to learn. In our case, we pay our students ten dollars an hour to attend a summer science camp. Attendance, willingness to participate, and excitement about being in class become the norm, not the laborious goal. We pay students to learn from professionals in real companies through summer internships. The combination of getting paid, earning credits, and working with real science and engineering professionals in a local company attracts and motivates students who most likely would never envision themselves in a STEM profession.

In both Algebra II and physics, we do not "dumb-down" the material. We choose to go more in depth to develop critical thinking skills rather than simply to expand the students' knowledge base. If students fail tests and classes because the subject is taught too fast, we slow down the teaching. Self-esteem and confidence are crucial to students' success. They are unlike my AP physics students whose confidence levels are on the other end of the spectrum and are perhaps too high and unrealistic. In my Algebra II class, building self-esteem and confidence through small, more frequent successes rather than fewer, large, high-stakes successes becomes critical. Practice tests with the same format as actual tests help build confidence by allowing students to judge for themselves what they have learned and to identify their weaknesses.

Treating these STEM students as special is also part of that self-esteem boost. Our field trips throughout the year serve several purposes. One is to expose the students to math and physics in settings outside the classroom and to enhance the classroom learning. Bonding with students, gaining new friends, and creating vivid memories add to the intangibles that boost self-esteem. Spending the money to buy lunches for the kids on these free field trips, providing them with a TI-86 calculator to use for the year, offering a science camp designed specifically for the program, and matching their interests and skills to available internships are also some of the important ways we build their self-esteem. These students may not feel good about themselves for many reasons beyond any teacher's control. So, even though I am not a great self-esteem builder based on my teaching style, the various enhancements provided for these students fill in that gap.

As part of this project, we also introduced a new Introductory Engineering course for twelfth graders. The course's major goal is to introduce the students to various STEM fields so that they can make a more informed decision about a field to pursue. When I was approached to teach the Introductory Engineering course, the principal told me that I would have a $130,000 budget to purchase materials. Introductory Engineering would replace the old woodshop classes. I did the research for the right kind of modular units and equipment, met with vendors, and made a proposal to the principal. Then budget cuts hit all schools, and my proposal was no longer viable due to its high cost. I still had to teach the course, but I had to scramble to piece together a course from the materials that already existed at LAHS. In the end, the course was not as effective as I had planned, and the first cohort of students felt let down. I had envisioned some truly powerful projects, but that was not meant to be. Teachers were being released; many courses were cut all across the curriculum, and my Introductory Engineering course suffered also. If the Regional Occupational Program (ROP) granted designation to the course, it would receive excellent funding, but without industry experience on my resume, I could not be credentialed as an ROP teacher. Thus, pursuit of the ROP designation and its funding was dropped. The district and school could offer only limited help in funding—certainly not enough to make an engineering class function optimally.

After discussion and collaboration with the Foothill/De Anza Community College District, a pre-engineering instructor from the community college provided an introductory college course in engineering that emphasized the different subfields within engineering and apprised students of the necessary academic preparation and requirements of each field. Within the context of tight budgetary constraints, a school may not be able to support fully the innovative technological methodologies of a costly course such as Introductory Engineering; consequently, the course may have to be taught more traditionally until such time as funds become available.

Another challenge we faced was low enrollment in the twelfth grade Introductory Engineering course. Students who entered the program knew that they had to sign up for the course, but because of factors in student schedules and parent decisions, many of the students in the second cohort did not enroll. Better counseling about the program to entering students and their parents will perhaps make this a non-issue in the future.

But for next fall when all 33 current first-year students move on to take the Introductory Engineering course, we still are faced with the issue of funding.

These students will have completed Algebra II, physics, a summer science camp, and possibly summer internships, and something will have to be done about the Introductory Engineering course to keep that excitement and vision of a STEM future at a high level. Too many times these students have been given promises, only to be let down due to "circumstances."

With a worthy vision and qualified people who support that vision at all levels, the problems will get worked out, and soon the rewards will be greater than the challenges. Tracking our students beyond high school will be another challenge, but it will be a challenge that will bring great rewards. We have just opened the door in our first two years. Some students are beginning to step through. Until they complete the journey and come back through to let us know where they end up, and we have data to track student success after high school, we will not fully see the greatest rewards from our program.

MORE FROM THE DIRECTOR'S PERSPECTIVE — ED LANDESMAN

Challenges

Adam and Leo have effectively discussed the challenges in planning and implementing the project from a teacher's point of view. As project director, I know the many difficulties of initiating and sustaining such a complex project with multiple major partners and diverse, changing personnel. Some of the challenges may be addressed pragmatically; others, however, involve the dynamic of the partnership. As I have already suggested, drawing on the expertise from all members of a partnership is crucial. Such commitment implies the respect for each person's capabilities and knowledge. While this may seem obvious, it is not always the case. There are instances in which a member of one component of a partnership may see him or herself as far more knowledgeable and hence may want to exert influence in a way that makes others feel a loss of dignity or control. One must continually be reminded of the different roles each partner plays and must bear in mind the varied challenges each must face. It is so easy to second-guess someone else's role and to "know how to do that person's job so much better than they do." For this reason alone, the choice of partners is critical. Many well-meaning and caring individuals may be capable of meeting the project's goals, but they may not be able to collaborate effectively and carry out the project's responsibilities as a team.

As an example, early on in this project, a key school district administrator strongly recommended several teachers as being ideal candidates for the project. Upon meeting these teachers and interacting with them, it was obvious that while these teachers were well-versed in their respective fields and were excellent teachers, they had so many other demands on their time and were involved in so many other activities at their school that their particular interest in our project was missing and their positive attributes would be of little or no value toward meeting the project's goals.

Similarly, in another project, some extremely well-meaning business executives were willing to offer financial resources, but they were able to spend little or no time working with the project team. And in higher education, some brilliant professors, who had the most honorable intentions of helping students succeed in learning, were unable to communicate with teachers in a way that made the teachers feel comfortable. These experiences have reinforced the importance of putting together a team with members who are willing to put in the time and who can respect and be respected by all participants. To bring together such a working team can often take as much time as it takes to carry out a major portion of the project itself. Yet without the appropriate team, the chance for success is greatly diminished.

Some of the key challenges to emerge in this project underscore what often occurs in the schools in the area of leadership. After I spent three years building working relationships with eight carefully chosen teachers, four principals, and five major administrators in three school districts, two of the teachers took on other responsibilities at their schools and consequently were unable to continue with their involvement in this project; two principals moved to other schools; and one principal and three district administrators retired. Consequently, we must identify new teacher partners, establish new working relationships, and build trust with about half of the key personnel. At times, such renegotiation of matching resources, building trust, and understanding project goals is like beginning the project anew. Even so, when we can demonstrate positive results in just a few years, the project can quickly draw in new participants who are willing to expend scarce resources to continue these worthwhile achievements.

Another major challenge has been obtaining suitable summer internships for students. When the project was first conceived, the financial state of the economy in local industry was relatively high, but two years later there was a dramatic dip. The buy-in of industry partners for mentoring students in the summer, independent of whether the student was funded or not, became an issue of a valuable time commitment and company resources. We solved that challenge this past summer by forming a "partnership" with the Industry Initiatives for Science and Mathematics Education (IISME). Previously, IISME worked with teachers, arranging internships for them in the summer and throughout the year. This extension to working with students represented a pilot project for IISME that, in addition to about half of the internships that I obtained, provided a database of internships that proved to be far better than we could have ever imagined. About 70 students were placed in internships at places including NASA/Ames, Lockheed Martin, Network Appliances, American Institutes for Research, Agilent Labs, WestEd, San Jose Technology Museum, Stanford University, Santa Clara University, Stanford Linear Accelerator Center, and UC Extension.

Rewards

Whatever rewards one might hope for from a project such as this one are best summarized in excerpts from a few of the unsolicited e-mails that I received following the science camp and internships. Any negative thoughts that go through my head on days when the project's challenges seem insurmountable are quickly counterbalanced when I receive letters such as the following ones. The letters remind me of the reason for our project: the students. The letters state:

> . . . you have given students like me this opportunity to discover our talents and make a possible career choice. There are no words that can truly express how thankful I am that you gave me this chance to grow and learn.

> . . . I enjoyed every moment of this summer with the engineering camp and the internship. I am considering an engineering career, and it is mainly because of you.

> . . . I never thought I could work at Stanford University and be able to work with professional and skilled people while I was still in high school . . . It encouraged me to take engineering in college and be more knowledgeable about the technology. And just to let you see what I was doing (together with another high school student) at SUMMIT/Stanford University, here is the link for the BAC simulator that we did with eighth graders as the targeted viewers: http://virtuallabs.stanford.edu/help/ BAC.swf. We (with the help of the staff of SUMMIT) did most of the layouts of the pages and a little bit of the animation. I learned a lot and had experiences, but also gained friends and confidence in myself. This is something I won't forget for my whole life.

❖ ❖ ❖

Commentary

MARGE CHISHOLM

Successful projects like the Collaborative for Higher Education High School Mathematics/Science Enrichment Project often appear to be easily implemented. All the right words are used in the overviews, i.e., "underrepresented youth," "enriched curriculum," "supplemental activities," and "partnerships." All the right ingredients are there. Yet, as so often happens when a project is successful, we may overlook what really made it happen. Ed Landesman? Adam Randall? Leo Florendo? NASA? CAPP?

So many successful elements went into this effort that it is hard to point to one and call it "essential." The three basic ingredients that made this project work—committed teachers, strong leadership, and partnership—are common factors that we already know are important. But we need to look deeper. We need to see *what* these teachers did; we need to understand *what* constitutes strong leadership; and we need to know *what* a partnership has to look like to make the difference.

Committed Teachers

Leo Florendo and Adam Randall are experienced physics and math teachers who have been an instrumental part of the project. They have taught all levels of students, and the teachers possess a keen understanding of the attitudes they would be facing when launching the project. As Adam observed, "Most students didn't see the usefulness of the interconnectedness of mathematics and science . . . (they) were simply going through the motions, trying to please me, the teacher, to get the highest grade for doing the minimum amount of work . . . They regarded adults and teachers who profess, 'Education is the key to success' or 'If you focus your mind, you can become anything your heart desires,' as lame and out of touch with reality."

Adam and Leo have a realistic view of students' lack of motivation and skepticism. They understand the environment so often found in high schools where a majority of students lack strong family, peer, or self-motivation to succeed academically. As the project began, the teachers realized that the fundamental key to making it work would be the student recruitment process. They had to become "academic detectives." They had to identify strategies to engage a population with weak study skills and low self-esteem related to achievement in math and science. Adam and Leo were fortunate in having the support of the administration, which provided a list of students who fit the underrepresented criteria. Adam and Leo shared the list of viable students with the students' previous math and science teachers, looking for evidence of underperformance due to lack of skills, not bad attitude. Eventually, they identified a core group of students they thought not only fit the underrepresented criteria, but also had the intellectual curiosity and ability to learn material well beyond their current academic placement.

How did these teachers get more than 50 teenagers to take time out of their busy lives to come and listen to why they should stop being satisfied with underperforming academically and start working harder than they had ever worked before? The teachers' success lay in the respect students had for them and their ability to connect with the students and motivate them to get involved in a challenging program. Secondly, Adam and Leo ". . . ordered pizza, lots of pizza, and invited them to lunch!" And, they made sure that scientists and engineers who visited the classes looked like the students. The teachers invited diverse role models, such as Hispanic and Middle Eastern engineers and astronomers and a female astrobiologist. The pizza presentation was a success and inspired many of the students to sign up for the project. However, some of the students who were invited did not even bother to come.

Undaunted, Adam and Leo launched the project. Along with conducting their regular classroom work, they planned trips, math and science summer camps, and new ways to integrate both the content and applications of physics and Algebra II. They engaged the students in meaningful work, collaborating on many levels and making strong connections between the concepts taught in Algebra II and physics. One teacher would reinforce an idea introduced in the other's class; sometimes they would switch classes, and Leo would teach a math lesson and Adam would teach a physics lesson. The students saw Adam and Leo as a team, and they explicitly experienced the integration of the two classes. It worked because both Adam and Leo have strong backgrounds in both math and science and because collaboration is natural for them.

The team and the teamwork have to be right. Ed Landesman believed it was vitally important to spend time working on getting the right team together. The chemistry of the teachers was one of the keys for success. Leo makes an important observation when he stated, "I know collaboration happens at other schools, too, but what makes our situation unique is that the communication between us is natural, and not forced due to the situation. Our . . . program would not be as successful were it not for the personal and professional relationship between Adam and me, a relationship that may not be measurable, but is essential to the program."

Leadership

Adam reflected that "As Ed continued to share his vision of the mathematics/science enrichment project and the commitment and resources given to the program . . . the feeling of support, understanding, shared vision, and leadership was inspiring. This was not someone's half-baked idea to improve standardized test scores of some of California's lowest achieving students. This was a well-planned, detail-oriented, highly connected project to give underrepresented students a real chance at positively changing their lives by earning a meaningful education."

Further, these two teachers believed that a good leader not only has to start the fire, but keep the fire burning strong. They made this observation about Ed: "I don't know anyone else who not only has the contacts in so many organizations in education and industry, but also has the knowledge, experience, savvy, courage, and respect to convince all of those partners to support [this] program."

On the other hand, Ed credited Leo and Adam with making the program successful. Additionally, leadership at the school needs to provide more than verbal support. Administrators or teachers in leadership roles must help identify students for the program, schedule the cohorts into the appropriate classes, orient and inform parents about the program, and sometimes fund supplementary materials and equipment. Key administrators at the district level may help address programmatic, personnel, budgetary, and public relations issues. And, of course, important components of the project depend on the visionary leadership of corporations/businesses and the scientific community that sees the value of substantively strengthening the educational connections between high schools and industry. At all levels, there must be mutual respect and willingness to listen to new ideas, revise strategies, and work together to achieve the project's goals.

Partnership

This project involves higher education, industry, and schools. Working closely together, the three partners not only engaged students in hands-on, meaningful work in the classroom, but exposed them to the real world of applied math and science. Making the leap between schoolwork and the real world happened through internships at various industrial sites and businesses. When presented with the end result or goal, students looked more closely, and considered more seriously, the steps necessary to realize their goals. This project included the essential part of the puzzle—providing a realistic path that students could envision for themselves and actually see that their goals were within reach.

The project "hooked" the kids on one integrated subject area, then provided them with powerful instruction in math and science and any needed support services. The project continued supporting the students through real-life experiences with business and industry internships, and then guided them through the college maze with the DEEP program. These kids will make the leap between school and the real world. They are gaining self-esteem and confidence; they are thinking about their future professional goals and realizing that these goals are within reach. This project provides an educational pipeline connecting students' aspirations in high school to a successful reality beyond college and university.

However, sustaining a successful partnership over time is not easy. The project director understands the importance of each partner being willing to commit time and energy over the long haul. For example, teachers must be more than highly qualified instructional leaders; they must have the time for this particular project. Many teachers have so many competing demands on their time that they cannot commit themselves wholly to a project that requires so much energy and time. Or a business partner might be willing to contribute funding, but not be committed to providing human resources or special activities. Again, choosing the right "partnership team" is critical.

Observations

It began as an idea . . . everyone has ideas. But the idea was nothing until the right people were tapped. Giving birth to an idea, like giving birth to a baby, requires concentrated effort. Like parenting, raising the idea to toddlerhood gets tricky. This is when the challenges start emerging—when the baby starts getting a mind of his or her own and when the advice from others or from the child-raising books doesn't work out so easily. Good ideas, like the toddler, start stumbling and falling down when faced with new challenges to implementation. Adam, Leo, and Ed discovered that trying to get their baby off the ground involved facing the challenges of budget cuts, competition with other programs, and getting "buy-in" from colleagues. The fact that these three men were able to address these challenges only proves the project's strength.

As the project expands to more high schools, it will inevitably experience growing pains and have to respond to critical child development questions: How will the youngster relate to the world? How will you keep the youngster's interest? How many times do you let a toddler fall down before you change tactics? What do you do to keep interest alive as a child moves into the teen years? How do you get kids to think about their futures? When and how do you revise expectations and find realistic answers?

Like good parents, Adam and Leo learned that they had to take innovative and sometimes risky steps to grow the concept and take it to the next level. They sometimes reminded themselves to do things differently, like remembering not to answer questions in the traditional "teachers have all the answers" mode. They realized that what worked in the beginning might not be feasible later; for example, internships available one summer might not be available the next year, and new internships would need to be found. They found that teenagers must "figure things out on their own," and Adam and Leo incorporated project learning and technological tools as often as possible into the curriculum to stimulate student interest, develop higher-order thinking, and promote collaborative investigations and discovery.

As the project progresses, each phase is somewhat experimental, and the project's architects, players, and parents must be vigilant about evolving needs to ensure that it can adapt while maintaining programmatic integrity. This project was born, raised, and pushed into adulthood through the team's unfailing confidence. However, the project's sustainability remains to be seen. It will need to become part of the school culture, woven into the basic instructional philosophy if it is to survive when special funding is no longer available.

Replication

Perhaps this project's biggest challenge and greatest value will be the ability to replicate it. As was true of initial implementation, replication will depend on putting together the right people: the team of able teachers, the project director who developed and refined the program, and the partners who know the pitfalls and the practices that work. They are in the best position to help put together other teams, to identify other teachers and leaders and business partners who could make it work in their own environs. The project director and teacher team might design professional development to help others understand the program components, the implementation process, and foreseeable challenges.

Additionally, this project succeeded largely because of the high degree of professionalism and commitment of the individual partners. It remains to be seen how much of its success is due to Ed Landesman's leadership and industry connections, how much is due to exemplary teachers like Leo and Adam, and how much is due to the climate at a particular school. Successful and effective replication will require identification of the program's essential components that must be retained, regardless of leadership and teachers involved. The project must be strong enough to survive without these particular players and yet retain programmatic integrity.

❖ ❖ ❖

Commentary

DAVE JOLLY

California's political, business, and academic leaders agree that our future economic strength and social cohesion depend on the workforce being more diverse and more highly educated. This model math/science enrichment project demonstrates that we can succeed in providing higher levels of education to our increasingly diverse population. High school teacher Leo Florendo aptly described this project as a "pipeline to the future" for his students. From CAPP's perspective this program addresses California's future needs and serves the aspirations of our high school students.

CAPP's continued support for this program is based on its measurable impact on high school students. In four years the program has had a direct impact on 250 high school students in four high schools, convincing them to enroll in Algebra II and physics and then by expecting and supporting rigorous academic work. As a result these students realized that the study of mathematics and science was not beyond them. This realization was an important change in perspective, since most of the students shared the misperception that only naturally gifted students can master these subjects and be eligible for jobs and college study that rely on these skills.

This program targeted students who were on the high school "default track," i.e., they cruised through high school taking easy courses that did not demand much student work. They had completed Algebra I and geometry with about a C average. They had more than met their high school mathematics requirement and would therefore take the path of least resistance and not enroll in Algebra II or a challenging science course like physics.

The efforts of teachers in this program like Leo Florendo and Adam

Randall provide a heartening example of the power of teacher enthusiasm for mathematics and physics and high expectations for students. One measurable result at each of the four participating high schools is that one additional section of Algebra II and physics was created and filled with juniors who had not seen themselves as math or science students and who would not have enrolled in these courses without encouragement, cajoling, and support.

Another important impact of this program has been to boost the number of Hispanic students in mathematics and science. Hispanic students in the East Side Union High School District made up slightly less than 40 percent of Algebra II students. In contrast, Hispanic students made up nearly 80 percent of the students in the project's Algebra II class.

Creation of additional classes was an early measurable success indicator for the program. Over the ensuing four years, rigorous and engaging classroom teaching, summer science camps, internships, and visits to colleges and business and government technology complexes all contributed to achieving a major goal of the program: preparing more students with an interest in mathematics and science for entry into college. When the project was extended to two high schools in the East Side Union High School District, typically, about 65 percent of the students from Yerba Buena and James Lick High Schools enrolled in two- or four-year colleges after high school graduation. So far, the college enrollment rate for students who have participated in this program is nearly 90 percent.

A significant reason for this program's success is Project Director Ed Landesman's understanding of the importance of involvement and buy-in of teachers, the school/district administrators, industries, and colleges. The partnership among these entities enables successful student recruitment, strong classroom instruction, and meaningful outside support through summer science camps, internships, and college and business visits. Collaboration among the partners fosters further enthusiasm among the teachers, whose curriculum and teaching practices are the most important ingredients in student learning.

CAPP believes this math/science enrichment model, as well as many of its components, can be replicated successfully in other high schools. The program started at two high schools and then was replicated in two additional high schools. The expansion schools were selected because they were low-performing high schools with many challenging students. Replication of this model and its various components, particularly in low-performing high schools, is the goal of CAPP's support for this mathematics/science enrichment project.

Some comments about cost may be helpful. CAPP's grant was to support start-up, development, and operational costs for three years. Costs per year to start and support two schools totaled between $100,000 and $125,000 per year. Strengthening the curriculum and alignment of Algebra II and physics takes time on the part of the teachers involved. Paying teachers for several weeks each summer and for time during the school year is, therefore, an important investment. Having a part-time project coordinator who can arrange and coordinate internship opportunities and the summer science camp and who can be the liaison between the teachers, principals, and district and business partners is essential. The project also shared costs for some internships, some of the summer science camp activities, and for student transportation to colleges and businesses. In most cases, as the school and district saw the success of students in the program, they worked out ways to absorb these costs using summer school funding, district transportation funds, and curriculum improvement resources. Partnerships with higher education institutions and government and business organizations also provided important in-kind services and support.

In retrospect, two aspects of this work underlie the student success and the program's adoption by schools and districts. First, the institutions and individuals developed a partnership around the shared goal of improving student access to and success in higher-order mathematics and science. Project Director Landesman was effective in helping the partners understand the benefits (both for their organization and for the students) of buying into the project and goals. Second, supporting the teachers enabled them to strengthen their curriculum and teaching practices. The program's summer opportunities and college and business visits helped engage the students, but rigorous instruction by knowledgeable teachers was essential.

This project has helped more high school students recognize that mathematics and science can be their pipeline to the future. It has opened rigorous math and science instruction to Hispanics and other underserved students—an essential outcome if our schools are going to meet the demands of industry for highly skilled professionals. For all of us, the project highlights the importance of providing challenging instruction for all students and eliminating the "default track" in our high schools.

Reinventing High Schools . . .
One Deep Conversation at a Time

NINA MOORE

IMPROVING HIGH SCHOOLS, reforming high schools, restructuring high schools, dividing high schools into small learning communities, sanctioning low-performing high schools. What should we to do with high schools? Nina Moore discusses the complexities of her work with four high schools over a six-year period and her efforts to support these schools as they struggle to overcome the forces impeding progress in traveling the often bumpy road to improvement.

❖ ❖ ❖

> The truth is that we don't know how to educate all students to these
> high academic standards. We never have. And so the system is not
> "failing." It is obsolete. It needs to be reinvented, not reformed.
> (Wagner, 1994, p. 309)

Schools in this country have always been the focal point for our most heartfelt dreams as well as our most severe condemnations. Education holds the promise of a better life, improved social status, and many professional opportunities for those who successfully move through the pipeline. Schools are expected to educate, socialize, democratize, and produce model citizens capable of fueling the local, national, and international engine that keeps America competitive in the global social and economic order. But as we have seen over time, schools have yet to live up to all of these expectations. Each new era resounds with calls for changes in the curriculum, teaching strategies, and governance structures in an attempt to satisfy the multiple purposes, roles, and responsibilities we expect schools to fulfill.

These tensions have been most prevalent in high schools. Prior to 1900, very few people even attended high schools. Many people have argued that secondary schooling was unnecessary because entry-level jobs were plentiful, and few employers required a high school diploma. In the twentieth century, as high schools became *the* place for preparing and sorting individuals for higher education and more advanced employment, the debates about the role and purpose of secondary schooling raged. Should high school provide the same curriculum for all students? Should everyone take rigorous academic courses or should vocational coursework be available for those not planning to go to college? The answers to these questions depended on whom you were asking, and the answers changed over time.

The debates continue with calls for national standards and a federal law pushing schools to leave no child behind and provide rigorous education to *all* children. In California, despite several years of accountability and reform initiatives, achievement at the high school level remains extremely low (notwithstanding significant improvement in elementary and to some degree middle schools). Unlike the situation prior to 1900, the need for high school graduates who are prepared to compete for limited spaces in postsecondary education and to be successful in an increasingly technological workforce is critical today.

This case study focuses on four high schools that were part of a special California Academic Partnership Program (CAPP) initiative designed to improve teaching and learning at underperforming schools. I describe the initiative's background, the schools that participated, and the work. My story examines the interactions between essential elements of school change, with a focus on changing classroom practice and, ultimately, improving student achievement.

THE CAPP PARTNERSHIP INITIATIVE

To understand this negative achievement trend in high schools despite myriad reform efforts and to identify what it takes to improve teaching and learning in low-performing high schools, CAPP established the

CAPP Partnership Initiative (CPI) in 1999. The initiative is a case study project with a limited number of schools designed to examine what we can learn about change at high schools, particularly how to move from low performing to high achieving. Schools that often need the most assistance either do not apply for external grants or are not competitive when they do apply. We felt a different approach to working with the newly identified Academic Performance Index (API) 1 high schools might reveal potential solutions to some of the intractable problems facing them. Rather than imposing a "program" or "strategy" to "fix" the achievement problems, the selected CPI schools were responsible for identifying and implementing strategies to improve academic achievement.

Utilizing the 1999 API rankings, CAPP identified approximately 15 high schools in the bottom API decile. The primary criterion for inclusion in the CPI project was the principal's expressed interest to partner with CAPP and engage in school reform. Secondarily, we wanted demographically diverse (e.g., size, geographic, socioeconomic, racial/ethnic) schools. We chose five schools. Since we were also interested in learning more about the challenges involved in working in a district, we agreed to work with two schools in Inglewood Unified School District (IUSD). The five schools included four urban and one rural school, two schools in the southern part of the state, two in the Central (San Joaquin) Valley, and one in northern California. When we established the CPI, the original five schools ranged in size from 670 to 2,682 students all with significant numbers of students traditionally underrepresented in postsecondary education.* Because the school with the largest population of the original group only participated in the Initiative's first three years, it is not discussed here. Table 1 provides some demographic information about the four schools included in this study followed by a brief description of each school.

McClymonds High School (MAC) is a small comprehensive high school in a large urban school district in northern California. Unlike the current small schools movement, MAC is not intentionally small. Rather, it is significantly under-enrolled, with an average enrollment of 700 over the past six years, but with a capacity of 1200. The school is situated in an economically depressed area fraught with significant drug and crime activity. The neighborhood is home to some of the poorest families in the region. Almost 60% of the students are eligible for

---

*Enrollment fluctuated at all the schools during the course of this project.

CPI SCHOOLS' ENROLLMENT DATA[1]

High School	Total Enrollment 2003–04	African American	Hispanic/ Latino	English Learners
McClymonds [2]	745	79.5%	9.7%	10.1%
Inglewood	2,111	46.9%	51.7%	23.1%
Morningside	1,585	39.8%	58.5%	31.2%
Orosi [3]	801	0.1%	89.8%	39.6%

1. Data in this table are from the California Department of Education, retrieved from http://www. ed-data.k12.ca.us.
2. 7.7% Asian student population not included in the chart. No other ethnicity more than 1%.
3. 6.7% Filipino student population not included in the chart. No other ethnicity more than 1%.

free and reduced-priced meals* and just under 70% receive CalWorks support. In 2002, 50% of the city's 113 murders took place within the attendance boundaries of MAC. For many students who live in this neighborhood, the school itself is the only safe haven. In fact, once you step onto campus, you become part of the MAC family.

Inglewood High School (IHS) and Morningside (MHS) are in a large urban area in southern California. Both schools are directly under the flight path of Los Angeles International airport. The roar of jets flying over the schools interrupts teaching throughout the day. A significant amount of violence and gang activity occurs in the surrounding community, and this violence sometimes spills onto the school grounds. Although they are within the same district and an eight-minute drive of each other, the tensions between the two schools were striking when the CPI project began. There was no communication between teachers or administrators and no common curriculum; they used different textbooks for the same courses, and personnel at MHS often felt that the district favored IHS.

In contrast to these urban schools, Orosi High School (OHS) is situated in a very small rural farming community. The high school serves two unincorporated towns with a combined population of fewer than 10,000 people. Hispanic farmworkers make up a majority of the community, and the poverty rate is around 90%. Over 90% of OHS students are eligible for free and reduced-price meals. While one may

*According to school personnel, this number is significantly underreported and is likely closer to 80-90%.

not expect the kind of violence in this area, the school erected ten-foot-high fencing all around the campus to keep gang members out. This community's isolation is palpable.

Well over three quarters of the students in all of four of these schools were testing at basic, below basic, and far below basic at all grade levels in algebra and English-language arts on the California Standards Test; and a majority were in the below and far below basic categories. All the schools had an API ranking of one when the project began, and they remain in the bottom decile. There has been some movement within the similar school rankings, but all still rank below a six (on the ten point API) when compared with similar schools. As part of the state's accountability measures, these schools also participated in the state-sanctioned Immediate Intervention/Underperforming Schools Program (II/USP).

The CPI Work

Holding the schools responsible for identifying their own improvement strategies did not mean there would be no guidelines or expectations for engaging in the change process. Given the conditions at these schools, as with most low-performing schools, CAPP had some concerns about their capacity to effectively spend the grant funds, particularly with the initiative's open-ended approach. While the schools would have quite a bit of flexibility, we did want some control over how they used CPI funding. So, unlike traditional grant programs the funding was not awarded to the schools up front. Rather, CAPP provided up to $150,000 per year, per school, for three to five years* to support activities as they were developed and implemented.

Once CAPP secured a commitment to engage in the initiative from the principal or district representative and established formal agreements, the important process of negotiating entry into the schools began. All of these schools had seen their fair share of reform efforts, from the imposition of state-level initiatives, standards, curriculum, and accountability systems to outside "providers" coming in with a program or strategy to "fix" the achievement problems, improve instruc-

---

*In the early years, CAPP provided three-year grants. However, after a decade of funding partnerships we recognized that it generally takes at least three years for schools and their partners to effectively work together and to implement activities in a systematic manner. Currently, most of our grantees are funded for up to five years with the proviso that they are making some progress along the way and that we are continuing to learn something from the projects.

tion, increase college eligibility rates, and boost parent and community involvement. In short, the schools were familiar with every reform flavor of the month. In the face of this historical and very real, skepticism, the CPI's intent had to be carefully and continually explained. This step required (and continues to require) time to build and sustain trust, identify key individuals willing to engage in the change process, and establish appropriate leadership structures for teachers to engage their colleagues in shifting the school's practice and culture.

The CPI work began with a self-assessment of the strengths and challenges at each school. The idea was to build on existing strengths, provide financial resources for those activities the school or district was unable to subsidize, and help coordinate existing efforts to avoid duplication of existing professional development and other support services. We agreed that the CPI activities would focus on fully implementing the state academic content standards, preparing students to pass the California High School Exit Exam (CAHSEE), and improving overall student achievement. Within the framework of these broad statewide goals, the schools were free to explore how to organize their work in ways they felt made the most sense.

Each school's self-assessment took a slightly different form with one important common feature: teachers and administrators were integrally involved in the assessment process. MAC's existing leadership team was composed of teachers from all academic disciplines and the two (at the time) administrators. During the first six months, the Leadership Team identified a long list of the school's challenges as well as strengths. We spent a significant amount of time together discussing the most pressing issues and how the school, with CAPP support, could address the challenges.

Because IHS and MHS were included together as a district initiative, a number of individuals were involved in the initial discussions, including mathematics and English teachers* from both schools along with the two principals, district representatives, and individuals from a local university.† Similar to the situation at MAC, this group spent the first six months reviewing strengths and identifying challenges. A formal Steering Committee‡ was established with mathematics and English

---

*To make this partnership manageable, we agreed to initially focus just on mathematics and English.

†UCLA had an existing partnership with this district and the two high schools.

‡In CPI's second year, we renamed this group the Leadership Team to formalize the teachers' leadership roles and responsibilities.

teachers from each school, the two principals, CPI coaches, and district Curriculum and Instruction Department representatives.

OHS had just completed a Western Association of Schools and Colleges (WASC) accreditation review and was already engaged in the planning phase of II/USP when the CPI began. An existing action planning team (including teachers, administrators, and parents) served as the primary focus group for the WASC process, which then continued to meet as part of the II/USP process. The II/USP required schools to work with an external evaluator to assess areas of need and develop an implementation plan to improve academic achievement.

The results of the self-assessment yielded three common themes across all three* sites as well as some unique activities. The common themes included time for collaboration, professional development, and support for leadership teams. Additionally, at MAC and OHS, the CPI supported a parent involvement component to increase parental engagement. OHS also developed a counseling program for incoming ninth graders and their families to set the tone and expectations for the high school experience. Unique to the district partnership with IHS and MHS, the CPI funding supported coaches in mathematics and English-language arts. I will describe some of the work at each of the sites in more detail to illustrate the CPI work.

MAC: After six months of Leadership Team ruminations about how to address Mac's achievement problems, the teachers decided to engage in professional development one Saturday per month, from 8:30 a.m. until 3:00 p.m., throughout the school year. Over the past six years these sessions included both teacher-led and outsider presentations on a wide range of topics from instruction and assessment to school climate and student activities. One year the group started a book club, and each Saturday session began with a discussion about the selected book and its implications for teaching at MAC. During the II/USP process, Saturday sessions became a key component of the school's Quality of Teaching Initiative, and they remain central to the school's professional development. When the school was going through the first phase of reorganizing into two small autonomous schools, the Saturday sessions provided an outlet for staff to express their fears, frustrations, questions, and concerns about "breaking up" the MAC family. About 90

---

* For this discussion the two schools (IHS and MHS) in the same district are treated as one project.

percent of the staff regularly participated in these professional development sessions.

In addition to the content, teachers looked forward to this time
together, something rare in the normal course of a teacher's day.
Participants shared that the Saturday professional development sessions
allow them "to grow professionally;" and gave them an "opportunity to
work together and learn." They said that the sessions "rejuvenate [their]
spirits because [they] can get worn down;" and their "day can become
very insular, so it is nice to see and be part of the community."

The CPI also supported the Leadership Team providing stipends to
participants for two-hour monthly meetings after school. The group
was responsible for making decisions about the content of professional
development sessions and other instructional and school climate issues
to improve teaching and learning. It was often a struggle to get active
participation from all the members, and I noticed most were watching
the clock, ready to leave halfway through the scheduled time (4:00–
6:00 p.m.). By the second year, the teachers took a much more active
role in setting the agenda, facilitating the meetings, taking notes, and
often not leaving until 7:00 or 8:00 p.m.

An annual retreat just prior to the opening of school is also now part
of the CPI activities. This event is held off site and allows certificated
and classified staff and partners* to engage in community building and
instructional planning in an atmosphere that teachers rarely experience
together.

IHS and MHS: As mentioned, the historical tension within the district,
particularly between IHS and MHS, was cited as these schools' most
critical challenge. The team of mathematics and English teachers, principals, and district representatives that met initially to conduct the self-
assessment agreed that the first activity should be a retreat away from
the district and city to strategize on ways to address this challenge. All
mathematics and English teachers from both high schools were invited
to attend the retreat. The two major recommendations that emerged
were time for professional development with teachers from both schools
and on-site mathematics and English coaching support.

The CPI funding supported monthly† joint department meetings

---

*Over the six years, university, community, support providers, and other partners
have participated in the retreat.
†During the fourth year we eliminated sessions in December, May, and June because
of low participation due to vacations, and testing.

that bring together English and mathematics teachers from both sites to discuss content and instructional issues. The meetings alternated between the two sites, and both content area groups met at the same time but in separate rooms. During years four and five, these joint meetings expanded to include middle school mathematics and English teachers.* A mathematics and a language arts coach provided on-site support to teachers at both schools and facilitated the joint department meetings.

Participants reported that the joint professional development sessions were invaluable in building collegial relationships between teachers at the two high schools and provided useful instructional strategies. Common assessments, pacing plans, and strategies were developed, and both schools now use the same textbooks. For the mathematics teachers the connection extended beyond the formal joint meetings. Teachers from both schools met for dinner approximately once a month on their own time.

The following example from conversations with individuals illustrates the impact of the CPI support on these two schools:

> At the beginning of year four, the teachers were experiencing problems with their contract and tacitly agreed to avoid any extra duty assignments until the agreement was settled. At the first joint department meeting, one math teacher explained to me that she and others chose to attend this session, despite the contract problems because they "like CAPP" and appreciate the CPI activities. (Personal notes from a site visit, 2003)

In 2004, CAPP administered a survey to collect feedback from teachers regarding how they felt about CAPP's professional development and coaching support. When asked to explain how the professional development sessions were helpful, teachers responded in the following ways:

> I had returned to the teaching field after many years of absence, so I was in great need of current effective educational practices. These sessions are packed with useful material and strategies.

> Most of all, the sessions got me to thinking about my classroom and how to improve my approach to instruction. I think I have grown during this time rather than becoming a fossil.

---

*Some of these are articulation meetings with both middle and high school teachers together, and in others they meet separately.

In response to a survey query about whether the professional development sessions improved the collaboration between middle and high school mathematics and English teachers, one teacher said the following:

> The middle school teachers got an opportunity to hear some of the concerns of the high school teachers regarding the incoming freshmen students. The meetings were a big help in bridging the gap. Both parties walked away with a better understanding of the job that needed to be done and with attainable goals set by the group.

The CPI also supported two full-time coaches, one in English and one in mathematics, as well as a part-time mathematics consultant. These individuals (all had extensive teaching experience) provide on-site support to teachers in their classrooms, including observation and feedback, demonstration lessons, and instructional resources. In addition, they facilitated the joint department meetings. Feedback from the teachers, both veteran and new, indicated that the coaching support was also extremely valuable. When asked about the most useful aspects of the coaching they received, one teacher made the following comment:

> The most useful aspects of coaching [is] our one-on-one meetings. In this forum we are able to benefit from their expertise and tailor it to our class needs. Many times coaches have multiple resources.

OHS: OHS was one of those schools that welcomed virtually every reform flavor of the month. The challenge here was the lack of coherent or consistent implementation of any one (or more) of the initiatives towards a particular goal or set of objectives. While there was agreement that achievement in mathematics and English was unacceptably low, it was extremely difficult to get consensus on how to improve performance in these areas. Some teachers believed professional development support would help; others believed that the current staff possessed the requisite skills and strategies to address the achievement problems, and more consistent implementation was all that was necessary; and still others believed there was no need to change their instruction, judging that those students who were able to get it, would and those incapable, would not.

It was pretty clear from the outset that yet another large-scale reform effort would go nowhere. So, CAPP supported collaborative planning time for the English and mathematics teachers to begin aligning their curriculum with the state's academic content standards. A very narrow task with a specific focus might help to move things at this school. About half the English department took advantage of the time. However, the teachers worked individually on aligning their own courses with the standards with virtually no conversation about how their courses articulated with one another or how they could collectively improve teaching and learning in language arts.

The mathematics teachers,* on the other hand, spent ten days together aligning the pre-algebra and algebra courses with the standards, discussing common assessments, and developing a timeline for the year. As a result of this planning time, the math department chair noted that they "are teaching more," and the students are more comfortable. The teachers realized it was possible to cover all of the essential concepts in the standards if they followed the timeline developed by the group.

One of the encouraging outcomes of the work at OHS was the institutionalization of some CPI activities. In particular, a parent support initiative and a special ninth- and tenth- grade counseling component both began with CAPP funding and the school now fully supports them. Both of these activities emerged from conversations between the teachers and counselors about students' needs and challenges around engaging parents more fully in their children's education.

Learnings and Outcomes

After two decades of research and experience with instructional, curriculum, and whole-school reform projects in secondary schools, CAPP found that several elements are important to the change process. These essential elements include leadership; professional development; curriculum, instruction, and assessment; professional community; collaboration; student support; and family and community involvement. Clearly, there is significant overlap between the elements.

Current CAPP research focuses on whether all of these elements must be present to effect change, which are most critical, whether the degree of their implementation impacts the level of change, and whether the presence of certain elements compensates for the absence of others. For example, will a strong culture of collaboration among teachers make up for weak administrative leadership?

During the initial stages of the CPI project, four of these elements

---

*Four out of the five teachers in the math department participated in the planning time.

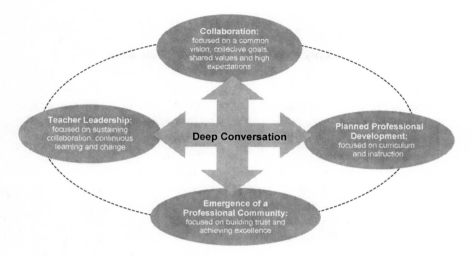

FIGURE I

seemed essential to beginning the school change process. Collaboration, professional development, professional community, and teacher leadership form a continuous and interactive loop critical to building an effective learning environment (see Fig 1).* At the center of this loop is what I call *deep conversation*, which is reflective dialogue about teaching and learning that provides a focus for and connection among sometimes disparate adults at the school (e.g., teachers, administrators, and counselors).

Figure 1 might raise a few questions, such as: Is there one entry point in this loop? Does the direction of the arrows make a difference? Do all four elements need to be present? Are certain elements more important than others? The simple answers are no, no, yes, and probably not. Change can begin at any of these points, though in some of the more challenging schools a robust professional community is not likely to exist. The arrows are simply intended to illustrate the dynamic nature of the change process, which is a continuous flow in both directions as

---

*While student support and parent and community involvement are also critical to improving achievement, the focal point of this initiative is on improving classroom practice and, therefore, it focuses primarily on the role of the adults in the school, particularly teachers. If rigorous, consistent teaching is absent, students will likely disengage from the learning process despite the support or number of interventions available to them.

well as in between the elements. All four elements need to be present, and therefore all are equally important.

However, the answers are not that simple and actually reside in the anchor point—deep conversation. It is not the required faculty or department meetings, the mandated professional development, the imposed programs, or leadership by default (i.e., no one else will step up, or someone is assigned to a job by the principal) that inspire meaningful change. It is the opportunities for professionals to engage in deep conversation about students, their learning, and effective instruction that is important for shifting a school's culture.

That said, while Figure 1 attempts to illustrate the interaction of the essential elements as a continuous loop, experience suggests that meaningful *collaboration* is often vital to initiating change, and it remains a key ingredient throughout the process. This collaboration requires those involved to agree on a common vision, goals, shared values, and high expectations, which requires more than cursory conversation.

If schools want *professional development* to focus on curriculum and instruction to improve teaching and learning, the activities should be organized around shared agreements to keep the work focused on curricular and instructional issues. One common trend in school improvement is the push for whole school reform, particularly in the lowest performing schools. This approach has forced many schools to adopt multiple programs, initiatives, and activities and attempt to implement all of them simultaneously. It is critically important for schools to identify one or two areas to focus on and begin implementation, recognizing that additional changes will flow simply from beginning the process. Here again, teachers need to engage in deep conversation about what kind of professional development is most effective for their children and themselves as professionals; simply choosing from a menu of one-shot workshops or programs that are "guaranteed" to "fix" the school is not enough.

With time, a community of professionals can emerge from the collaboration and professional development organized around instructional practice. This *professional community* allows for the sharing of best practices and an exploration into the more difficult issues surrounding the school community and change. The professional community provides a level of trust and a foundation for building a culture that supports rigorous teaching, high expectations, and nurturing the hearts, minds, and souls of all those inside the schoolhouse. Without this sense of community, collegial connection to one another, and the willingness to engage in deep conversations, individual practices may change, but deep structural change is unlikely.*

Closing the loop takes *teacher leadership* to sustain the collaboration, continuous learning, and community. Rather than being conferred by the administration, by virtue of position (e.g., department chair), or by default (no one else wants to be responsible), the kind of leadership necessary for real change emerges from and is informed by the looping process and anchor point conversations illustrated in Figure 1.

This notion of closing the loop implies a finite, perhaps even consistent process, where one element always follows another, and the relative importance of one over another can be determined and is always the same. It is virtually impossible graphically to represent the complex and dynamic nature of change that is taking place at the CPI schools. The important learning has been the presence (or absence) of deep conversations and interactions. All of these elements were present to some degree in all of these schools before the CPI. There were leadership teams, collaborations with universities and other partners, professional development activities, and pockets of reflective dialogue among colleagues. It is the deep conversations, oftentimes difficult for those who live in schools, that take place in a more systemic way that are critical to changing a school's academic, social, and cultural mores.

The absence of these elements in our schools is well documented. Nespor (1997) describes the "discontinuities" within educational organizations where units function independently despite their "symbolic and ceremonial" linkages. He argues that teachers have little sense of connection between what they are doing in their classroom and what goes on in other classrooms or other schools. In fact, Nespor (1997) notes that teaching at most schools is

> treated as a quality of individual teachers rather than of the faculty as
> a whole or of the relationships between teachers and the community.
> Although this definition might have suited teachers set in their habits, it
> created enormous problems for. . . . teachers who wanted to change how
> they taught but who had trouble finding opportunities for the conversa-
> tion and learning they wanted and needed (p.12).

Opportunities for "the conversation" and professional learning must be more than an inspiring speaker or an engaging workshop, even one

---

*For a discussion about deep structural change in schools, see Barbara Benhan Tye's article, "The Deep Structure of Schooling" in *Phi Delta Kappan*, December, 1987, pp. 281-284.

that provides strategies that teachers can use the next day in their class-rooms. Professional development must include deep reflection about the difficult or "undiscussable" issues related to school culture (Argyris, 1987). It must go beyond learning exemplary pedagogical skills and the most current content knowledge to an examination of fundamental beliefs and expectations about teaching and learning. Argyris posits that an "integral part of the culture of a school includes the factors that inhibit or facilitate the ability of members of that culture to reflect on and alter the culture" (p. 182). The CPI supports collaboration and professional development, fosters a professional learning community and leadership opportunities for teachers at the schools, encourages self-reflection and deep conversations, and engages a friendly outsider working inside to facilitate the change process.

Outcomes

Over the course of six years there were shifts in all of the CPI schools. Participants at all the sites reported that the opportunity to collaborate as professionals was CPI's most important component. Using the CAPP funds to pay stipends for teachers to work together outside of their regular contracted time facilitated this collaboration and engendered opportunities for deep conversation. The intent at all sites was to use collaborative time for professional development focused on instructional issues. While the content of these sessions varied across sites, and even within sites from one activity to the next, the opportunity to come together was seen as a benefit to all participants. This sense of community did not previously exist at any of the sites.

Collaboration, professional development, the evolution of a professional learning community, and leadership are clearly important to changing the culture of practice at each of the CPI sites; this is by no means a new idea in the study of school change. What is missing from the literature is that change happens one school at a time, and each site must go through its own process. Common elements, as outlined previously, must be present for change, but those inside the schoolhouse have to make sense of and own each step in the process. All of this requires time.

A number of challenges existed with the apparent inability of the schools to consistently implement the professional development activities, translate the strategies into a change in classroom practice, and sustain a sense of community. However, for each step backward there have also been important steps forward.

At MAC the nature of the dialogue among the staff changed. During the first year, most of the achievement problems were blamed on the students, the lack of preparation in earlier grades, the lack of parent involvement, and the poverty in the community. Then teachers started asking what they could do differently, and they took responsibility for their students' achievement. They considered themselves a family; yet when the school engaged in the small schools' planning process during the fourth year, many commented on the rift this created in the school. One person noted that "in some cases the cohesiveness that we've tried to build up for the last three or four years has sort of been shattered." Then at the final Saturday professional development session of year four, the staff acknowledged the fractures in the community and talked about accomplishments and plans for the following year, which focused on improving instructional practice, accountability, and student achievement.

IHS and MHS experienced five superintendents in the district, three principals at IHS, four principals at MHS, the death of the district Director of Curriculum and Instruction, and high teacher turnover all during CPI's first four years. Yet the joint department meetings created a collegial culture across the two schools that never existed in the past, and the sessions have become the district's primary professional development activity. Based on the CPI coaching support, two English teachers have moved into coaching positions at both schools to provide support for their colleagues, which is building capacity for on-site leadership and professional development.

Writing was targeted as a key area for improvement during the first two years of the CPI at OHS. At every meeting, the Curriculum Leadership Council (CLC) discussed strategies to help improve student writing, and agreed to implement these strategies schoolwide. While implementation was uneven, scores on district and state writing assessments have improved. On the other hand, despite the collegial collaboration with the mathematics department, achievement remained unacceptably low in that subject area. Yet discussions about standards-based instruction are now much more common across all subject areas. And, after four years of meeting and feeling like they had little or no power to make a difference, the CLC now appears ready to assume responsibility for change.

A leadership group was part of the work at each site, and these teams provide a forum for the members to explore issues related to instructional change, professional development, and what could be done to create an environment that supports student engagement and achievement. Leadership is a key component to sustaining the collaboration, professional learning, and community that is essential to school change. As with the other elements in the loop, the nature of leadership varies across the three CPI projects. All of the teams identified the professional development activities and instructional strategies they felt could make a difference, and the team members communicated the plans to their colleagues. In some cases team members even led or facilitated the activities.

Some of the participants' activities and roles did not initially appear to be the kind of "leadership" that would affect real change. However, while some "leaders" at all of the sites seemed reluctant to take responsibility and hold each other accountable for changing practice, all those involved *have* engaged in this CAPP Initiative and assumed roles beyond their regular duties as part of their "leadership" positions. For example,

> At OHS, the Curriculum Leadership Council often expressed a limited view of its power to implement changes; any real change would require the principal to take the necessary actions. By the end of year four, the group acknowledged they needed to meet more frequently and that if anything is going to change they would have to "take the bull by the horns" and make it happen. (Phone conversation with the project director, May 7, 2004.)

At all of the sites, the conversation has changed. A different level of dialogue focuses more on instruction, assessment, and standards as opposed to all the other "problems" with the children, the parents, the community, poverty, the lack of preparation and anything else external to the schools.

Challenges

My approach to this Initiative was based on three fundamental beliefs about school change. One, if collaboration is vital to the change process, meaningful collaboration, be it with an outside entity or internally to a school, must begin from wherever the school is. Two, imposing, or even offering, a program that will "fix" a school, no matter how effective the program has proven to be, will not create change. Three, teachers must be at the center of the reform initiative, and they must have the opportunity to assume leadership roles for change to actually happen. My naïve assumption was that an open and supportive approach would inspire the schools to engage in the change process, as though everyone was just waiting for the opportunity to engage in collaboration, deep conversations, and in-depth professional development, and jump into a leadership role, seize power, and change the conditions that led to low achievement at the schools. Lack of opportunity was the only thing holding them back.

My assumption about the process did not match reality. While some teachers welcomed the opportunity to engage in difficult conversations, participate in professional development, and assume leadership roles, others were more skeptical, resistant, or simply not interested. Despite their students' academic performance, the adults in the school community did not all agree on what the problem was or how to address it or even that there was a problem. Even when there was "agreement" about making a change, everyone did not necessarily follow through. There would be moments of real progress or movement as well as backsliding. The deep conversations, the professional development, the professional community, and the leadership opportunities did not necessarily translate into change in classroom practice. It became clear that significant changes would take time and require many deep conversations. This reflection about one Leadership Team meeting illustrates this learning.

> I was anxious about "implementing" or beginning the work so that we could demonstrate change as soon as possible. However, I realized during this first year the importance of allowing some discussions to run their course, even with what sometimes seemed like repetitive and duplicative comments. Often, the more the group talked, the more honest the discussion became, as evidenced by one discussion about low teacher expectations. It was not until all aspects of an issue were on the table that we began to get agreement that it was a problem and then get buy-in on ways to address the challenge. (Personal notes 2003)

A significant challenge was my own expectations about the nature and timing of change as well as teachers' level of engagement in the process. I assumed that given an opportunity, teachers would welcome the chance to engage in professional learning and take on leadership responsibilities; all they needed was time and compensation.* In actual-

---

*Compensation is always a contentious issue when working with teachers. I wanted to make sure that teachers were compensated for any additional time they spent on CPI activities to acknowledge their status as professionals.

ity, this is clearly an evolutionary process and a delicate balancing act. Teachers must continually walk the line between focusing on assessing and improving their own classroom practice, being a colleague, *and* pushing each other to change.

My impatience for the deeper school-level change increased my tendency to discount the significance of smaller changes along the way. Clearly reform is a continual process, and schools do not just arrive at deep structural change simply because there is a process in place or a friendly facilitator to help move the process along. *All* of the incremental steps, both forward and backward, are important and necessary building blocks to more systemic change. The forays into deep dialogue about critical issues can just as quickly revert back to more surface behaviors, conversations, and practices.

There is a need for an "outside friend" who can provide a different perspective on the work and help keep the process moving. It does, however, require a great deal of patience and investment to build and sustain relationships. This is also a delicate balancing act—getting inside enough to develop the relationships and understand the context and conditions, but not so close that perspective is lost. Over time, I developed relationships with teachers, administrators, and classified staff at each site. These relationships are important for maintaining trust and allowing me to honestly reflect back to individuals at the schools what I see going on or areas that need more attention. Many insiders talk to me about issues they would not necessarily share with colleagues.

Debates about the purpose of schooling have stimulated many reform efforts throughout history. What does a "changed" school look like? How do we know when we have succeeded? Educational change is essentially an organic and ongoing process of interactions among those inside the schoolhouse (teachers, students, and administrators) and the community (local, regional, national, and international) in which the school is situated.

The CPI project has allowed me to see just how complex and multi-faceted change really is and that there is no formula for working with schools. Despite the ultimate common goal to improve teaching and learning, my work with the CPI schools requires a personal commitment to honoring the complexities and each school's unique social, cultural, and economic context. While I can suggest that a school try monthly Saturday professional development sessions because they were effective at another school, ultimately that school will have to design and adapt professional development activities to meet its own needs.

This is a journey, a delicate dance of support, and at the same time an attempt to cocreate a vision for something different, for something more. It is an intricate balance of building trust and friendship, yet maintaining enough distance to do the "right" thing. The most vocal and the most powerful are not necessarily the best practitioners.

I am often asked, what difference have you made? Some days I feel confident about saying that CAPP, that I, was a part of realizing the emergence of some of these essential elements of change, e.g., professional development looks very different in all of the schools (and one district); there is a palpable sense of community in three of the schools where none existed previously; and collaboration time exists, is valued and, in some cases, is highly protected. Other days I wonder about the students who still perform below and far below basic on tests, who fail to pass the California High School Exit Exam, who are still not graduating, who graduate but do not have access to college, who disengage from the entire educational process. How do we reconcile the importance of this work (i.e., supporting schools and teachers) with these so-called "objective" performance measures? As my journey with the CPI project continues, I seek answers to this and the many other complicated questions that surround school change.

REFERENCES

Argyris, D. (1987). The ethnographic approach to intervention and fundamental change. In *Action Science*. San Francisco: Jossey-Bass
Nespor, J. (1997). *Tangled up in school: Politics, space, bodies, and signs in the educational process*. New Jersey: Lawrence Erlbaum Associates, Publishers
Wagner, T. (1994). *How schools change: Lessons from three communities revisited* (Second Edition). New York: RoutledgeFalmer

❖ ❖ ❖

Commentary

JON WAGNER

Research on school change has been dominated by questions about how externally designed policies and practices can be implemented effectively inside schools. This domination is reflected in a wide range of commentaries, case studies, and research reviews. Some key studies and statements that define this perspective appeared more than 20 years ago (see, for example: Berman and McLaughlin, 1975; Crandall and Loucks, 1983; Hall and Hord, 1984; Huberman and Miles, 1984). However, the allure of exogenous change strategies is well represented in current research and policy initiatives, including No Child Left Behind regulations and other large-scale reforms proposed since the mid-1990s.

The popularity of external change initiatives is understandable, in part because so many other dimensions of schooling are exogenous as well. Funding for public education comes primarily from outside local school communities, and the same is true for other components of formal schooling, including credentialed teachers, approved textbooks, and official assessments. If school operations rely on external resources such as these, then why shouldn't school improvements rely on externally designed change strategies? External change initiatives are a popular strategy for demonstrating that "action" has been taken to address schooling problems defined by state and national policy makers, and many people also see the initiatives as the only viable remedy for schools that seem unlikely or unable to improve on their own.

Despite their popularity and attractions, external change initiatives are always more complicated, uncertain, and arbitrary than their advocates suggest. It's difficult for such efforts to succeed without adjusting to local circumstances, for example, and either circumstances or adjustments sap reform vitality. Externally promoted school reform efforts can also miss their marks when the circumstances in which they were designed change before they can be fully funded or implemented.

Above and beyond these challenges, the success of reforms fashioned outside schools depends in large part on people who work inside and whose contributions vary according to the varied infrastructure, past practice, leadership, and culture of individual schools. As a special case of this variation, school staffs can be more or less resistant to externally initiated programs of whole school change. Indeed, neglecting these internal elements has jeopardized more than a few grand plans for improving the schools (for thoughtful treatments of this issue, see Fullan & Stiegelbauer, 1991; and Sarason, 1982).

For all these reasons, acknowledging the importance of a school's internal change process—as either an adjunct or alternative to external change initiatives—has much to recommend it. But initiating change from inside the schools has complications of it own.

As reported in some studies (Corbett et al., 1984; J. Wagner, 1998; T. Wagner, 2000), the story lines for internally initiated school change are more complex and more difficult to follow than what we've come to expect from studies of policy or program implementation. Even when internal change initiatives contribute directly to school improvements, they typically implicate so many variables that they're difficult to assess. Research about internal change strategies is also fragmented and somewhat incidental, in part because changes that unfold independent of visible policies or programs are sometimes difficult to notice, follow, or record. As a disconcerting backdrop to these issues, when schools are already headed in the wrong direction, staying the course of their internal change process can make matters even worse.

Taken together, these considerations suggest the value to school improvement of articulating external and internal change initiatives. But what forms of articulation work best for low-performing schools? Does diminished instructional capacity go hand in hand with a school's diminished capacity for planning and supporting change? If so, are there ways to address both academic and planning deficiencies simultaneously? If not, what should come first? And how can outside support stimulate (rather than stifle) the kind of critical, internal inquiry that's necessary to support and guide whole school change?

Nina Moore's account of trying to jump-start schoolwide change in several low-performing schools provides a framework for developing better answers to these questions. Her analysis starts by recognizing that, first and foremost, schools are places where people come to work. As a routine feature of this kind of work, both teachers and administrators develop and change standard school practices. These practices make school reform difficult, but the power of teachers and administrators to change them makes it possible. On a school-by-school basis, for example, teachers and administrators can alter how they engage students in academic work, conduct faculty meetings, manage school-community relations, hire or assign teachers, and so on. With this discretion in mind, the key question is not whether change is possible, but rather what it takes for changes to lead toward improved student outcomes.

As one step towards answering this question, Moore has proposed a framework for thinking about the improvement potential of internal change processes in low-performing schools. Key elements of this framework include schoolwide collaboration, teacher leadership, and curriculum-based professional development. Moore argues that under the best circumstances, these elements can come together within deliberate and effective efforts to improve school outcomes. When they do, adjustments that fall within the routine purview of teachers and administrators can become vitalized as school change tools. As these tools become more familiar to school communities, discussions about how work is done in schools can themselves become an engine of whole school improvement.

Some reform advocates might be tempted to invest exclusively in one element of Moore's framework and let the others slide, but that runs counter to an important lesson she gleaned from working with several low-performing schools: the value of each element depends in part on all the others. Some schools might have strong teacher leaders but lack the kind of collaboration necessary to problem-solve specific change strategies. Others might have thoughtful professional development programs but lack teacher leaders who can mobilize their colleagues into action.

Tying reform hopes to any one dimension of Moore's framework is problematic for another reason: the potential for whole school change is shaped not only by all elements of Moore's proposed framework, but also by a school's distinctive reform history. After too many years of what Moore calls the reform "flavor of the month," for example, school members may be unwilling to embrace new change proposals, regardless of how promising they might be. And yet, schools isolated from these same reform initiatives may lack information about alternatives to their present policies and practices. To design and manage successful school change efforts, school differences of this sort need to be noticed and understood.

As a third caution, Moore notes that "it is the depth of each element that really matters" and that this can only come "from deep and ongoing dialogue about what will improve teaching and learning." Moore's account illustrates how this kind of dialogue can evolve from modest and prosaic points of departure and how, once established, it can help school members plan and solve problems, build and extend leadership skills, and enrich schoolwide collaboration. Above and beyond these specific contributions, Moore identifies this kind of dialogue, or what she calls "deep conversation," as a crucible through which a school's culture can be acknowledged and refashioned. As she puts it:

It is not the required faculty or department meetings, the mandated professional development, the imposed programs, nor leadership by default . . . that inspire meaningful change. It is the opportunity for professionals to engage in deep conversation about students, their learning, and effective instruction that is important for shifting the culture of a school.

In placing "deep conversation" at the heart of the school change process, Moore's account encouraged me to reconsider a school change project I observed at Tree Creek School some years ago (J. Wagner, 1997, 1999) and a related project that Erickson and Chistman (1996) initiated with several low-performing Philadelphia schools. Within these two projects (each of which were coincidentally called "Taking Stock"), external consultants helped collect data about the expectations of school staffs and the activities in which they were engaged. These data were incorporated into schoolwide discussions that the consultants helped facilitate but did not direct. As these discussions became more and more rewarding to school staffs themselves, conversations also focused more directly on significant issues of teaching and learning, and that led school members to craft thoughtful new strategies for improving student outcomes. This process was characterized by stops and starts, but the face-to-face discussions I observed at Tree Creek enabled teachers and administrators to develop a kind of collective wisdom that ran "deeper" than the ideas individual school members came up with on their own.

This kind of deep conversation can serve multiple purposes, and Moore identifies a feature that gives them special significance in helping school members move from one stage of the change process to another. Because they are rewarding on their own terms, and not just a means to some other end, deep conversations can keep school members collectively engaged throughout the ups and downs of a school change episode. In this regard, the conversations are particularly important after initial enthusiasm has begun to fade and before reform implementation is stable enough to adequately assess.

The ambiguities and uncertainties of this kind of "dead space" in the practice of school reform get short shrift in the research literature and in professional lore, both of which are shaped by enormous policy pressures to quickly assess the relative merits of different reform strategies. But school improvements rarely happen quickly enough to generate confirming evidence when it's needed. And, even if early returns are favorable, empirical assessments of effectiveness can't be trusted until a program is relatively stable—or achieves what Tharp and Gallimore call a state of "ecological climax" (1979). Because they are engaging to school members even when a project is losing steam, going through rough spots, expanding or contracting, or undergoing revisions on the fly, deep conversation provide some of what's needed to bridge the gap between initial faith in a good idea and evidence that it might be good in practice.

In identifying deep conversations as part of what it takes for teachers and administrators to move their schools forward, Moore's account also reminds us that not all schools can start them up on their own. This recognition has led many educators to recommend exogenous over endogenous change strategies, but the balance Moore and her CAPP associates struck seems a better bet: schools received funds for specific change activities, based in part on how thoughtfully the activities had been developed and planned, but Moore also worked with schools to strengthen their capacity for thoughtful planning and development.

Moore notes that for many low-performing schools, initiating schoolwide deliberations of any sort can be a difficult first step. External support can help, but the most promising issues for stimulating such discussions vary from school to school, and some start-up issues can appear to outsiders as trivial or even counterproductive. Why hold meetings to discuss the bell schedule, for example, when half the kids are failing algebra? Why spend time helping seniors through graduation rehearsals when many juniors are poised to drop out?

The approach Moore recommends does not suggest that discussions about the bell schedules and graduation rehearsals will lead, on their own, to improved schooling. However, she does remind us that instructionally trivial issues can stimulate schoolwide conversations that focus eventually on instructionally significant issues. As a corollary to this process, Moore also notes that without deep conversations among teachers and administrators, it may matter little what school members do talk about.

By explicating her work as a thoughtful, "friendly facilitator," Moore's account confirms the value of external consultants in helping low-performing schools initiate a rewarding and promising process of internal improvement and renewal. The process itself is complex, incremental, and uncertain, and many reform advocates are eager to find something that is faster and more surefire, but I think Moore has it just about right: initiating and sustaining thoughtful change does depend on one conversation and one school at a time. Acknowledging this involves a substantial stretch for both external policies and internal school practice. By bringing that stretch more sharply into focus, Moore's account also brings whole school improvement closer into reach.

REFERENCES

Berman, P., & McLaughlin, M.W. (1975). Federal programs supporting educational change: Vol 5. Executive summary. Santa Monica, CA: The Rand Corporation.

Corbett, H. D., Dawson, J. A., & Firestone, W. A. (1984). *School context and school change.* New York: Teachers College Press.

Crandall, D. P., & Loucks, S. F. (1983). People, policies and practices: Examining the chain of school improvement, Volume X. *A roadmap for school improvement: Executive summary of the study of dissemination efforts supporting school improvement.* Andover, MA: The Network.

Erickson, F., & Christman, J. B. (1996). Taking stock/making change: Stories of collaboration in local school reform. *Theory into Practice,* 35(3), 149–157.

Fullan, M. G., & Stiegelbauer, S. (1991). *The new meaning of educational change* (Second ed.). New York: Teachers College Press.

Hall, G. E., & Hord, S. M. (1984). *Change in schools: Facilitating the process.* Albany, NY: State University of New York Press.

Huberman, M. A., & Miles, M. B. (1984). *Innovation up close: How school improvement works.* New York: Plenum.

Sarason, S. B. (1982). *The culture of the school and the problem of change* (Second ed.), Boston: Allyn and Bacon.

Tharp, R. G., & Gallimore, R. (1979). The ecology of program research and evaluation: A model of evaluation succession. *Evaluation studies review annual,* 4, 39–60.

Wagner, J. (1997). Discourse innovations in a restructuring elementary school: Alternative perspectives on linking research and practice. *Elementary School Journal,* 97(3), 271–292.

Wagner, J. (1998). Power and learning in a multi-ethnic high school: Dilemmas of policy and practice. *Ethnic identity and power: Cultural contexts of political action in school and society* (pp. 67–111). Albany, NY: SUNY.

Wagner, J. (1999). The pragmatics of practioner research: Linking new knowledge with power in an urban elementary school. *Elementary School Journal,* 100(2), 151–180.

Wagner, T. (2000). *How schools change: Lessons from three communities.* New York: RoutledgeFalmer.

The High School Instructional Leadership Initiative

KATE JAMENTZ

SIXTEEN HIGH SCHOOLS participated in the Instructional Leadership Initiative (ILI), focusing on mathematics and English departments. Teachers learned to "unpack" the standards to understand the demands of standards-based instruction, develop curriculum units and assessments, analyze student work, and strategize for re-teaching if necessary. In the process, departments discovered the power of collaboration, and teachers emerged as instructional leaders.

❖ ❖ ❖

I. AN OVERVIEW

The Western Assessment Collaborative (WAC) at WestEd designs and provides professional development to support the implementation of effective standards-based instruction and school practice. We set out to create professional development tools and services that help teachers and administrators understand what effective standards-based instruction entails, and then to consider what leadership and organizational practices are necessary to build and sustain these skills.

WAC's work argues that the call to teach all students to high standards requires instructional skills that were unnecessary in systems that assumed only some students could or would achieve to high levels. In standards-based systems, teachers must know how to target and differentiate learning opportunities so that each student can succeed. They must have, or be able to create, assessment tools that generate evidence of student progress and be skilled in interpreting the data or the student work diagnostically to target future instruction to individual needs (Jamentz, 2002). Teachers in schools committed to high achievement by all students must also have the time and skills necessary to collaborate with colleagues to establish shared expectations for student performance, to read and understand data about how students are progressing, and to work together to allocate resources to maximize student performance. Our work in high schools supports teachers in learning and doing these things.

Sixteen high schools sought support from WAC after receiving a grant from the California Academic Partnership Program (CAPP) "to support implementation of standards and improve student performance." CAPP grants are generally given to schools identified on the state accountability system as low-performing, but whose plans suggest promising effort to improve performance. Work with CAPP schools engaged teachers from mathematics and English departments. The project is known as the CAPP/WAC Instructional Leadership Initiative (ILI).

Whether our entry into high school work was motivated by an interest in developing standards-based instructional units or common assessments, professional development sessions focused on how these tools could be developed and used to focus attention on instructional improvement. Work in all schools focused on helping teachers to do the following:

- understand the cognitive demands of the standards they were required to teach
- design or select assessments that generated credible evidence of achievement of those standards
- negotiate a performance standard which specified the criteria that was expected of all students
- make a plan to provide all students access to instructional opportunities that would help them meet the criteria
- analyze student work diagnostically and plan for reteaching as necessary
- reflect on what support they need to maximize student success
- recognize effective standards-based instructional practices and begin to incorporate them into their practice

Participating teachers created assessment tasks to be given by all teachers teaching a given course, the scoring guide for that assessment, and guidelines for the instructional opportunities that must be provided to students to prepare them to do well on the assessment. The teachers who authored this original assessment and instructional unit plan then engaged colleagues in teaching the unit, giving the assessment, negotiating a shared performance standard, and analyzing the resulting data to understand what actions they might take to improve student performance.

WAC services were designed as performance-based professional development. Participants were expected to produce a unit that met specified performance criteria and to do so on a timeline so that feedback could be provided on the work-in-progress.

Workshop sessions, which might convene leaders from several schools and several departments at a time, provided models and guided practice of new skills. On-site visits provided support for application of these skills by individuals in each school. In addition, WAC facilitated cross-school feedback sessions where project participants critiqued each other's work, as well as external reviews of the instructional units by content area experts. The unit development timeline included time to revise the unit based on feedback from content experts or teachers from other schools.

Impact on Instructional Skills and Department Practice

To determine the impact of the Instructional Leadership Initiative on teaching, we looked at what teachers in our projects learned as the result of their participation, the ways in which project participation did or did not affect individual classroom practice or collegial department-level work, and the conditions within the school or project design that contributed to improvements in practice at the classroom and school level.

We reviewed and analyzed drafts and final versions of instructional units produced and interviewed key teacher leaders. To understand the project's influence on departments, we conducted a self-study session involving teams from participating departments where they shared department practices and evaluated their own progress. Many project participants shared the view that the project served as a powerful professional development experience.

> This has been the most important professional development initiative I've seen in years. It addresses the things we never address . . . what happens

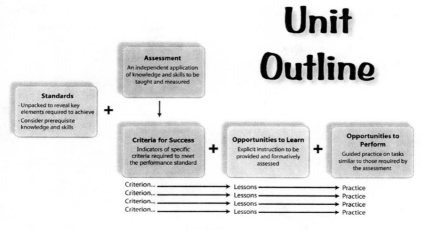

FIGURE I

in classrooms . . . by helping teachers to refine lesson plans and think differently about what they teach. (Principal from participating school)

I have a very, very young department. I have only two people who have been here more than three years. I also have a mandate from the district to align our curriculum with standards immediately, if not sooner . . . the work with WestEd and CAPP has given invaluable staff development in the area of how to make standards alignment . . . happen in classrooms. This is the most valuable staff development experience I have had personally in many years. It is incalculable what it is doing for us here on our campus. (English Department Head)

Beyond these testimonials, units and assessments produced by participating teachers provided evidence of the increasing ability to develop or identify rigorous assessments and plan for adequate instruction. During each of the first two years of the project, draft units were submitted to reviewers, including content experts. Assessments and units were scored on a four-point scale, and feedback was provided about strengths and deficiencies. Scoring criteria included these:

· the alignment of the assessment to the standard
· the degree to which the unit provided evidence of appropriate content knowledge
· the clarity and comprehensiveness of the criterion on which student work would be judged
· the comprehensiveness of the recommended lessons to prepare students to meet the performance criteria

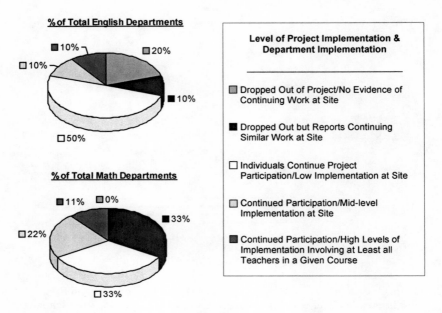

FIGURE 2

Teachers then had the opportunity to revise the unit in relation to the feedback.

In addition to the instructional planning and design skills exhibited in the unit's revision, some teachers began to surface and expand their expectations for student performance and make clear connections between their own instructional practices and what students were able to do. In some schools, teachers were better able to focus their collaboration on classroom practice and develop personal and collective accountability.

But, despite very real progress for some teachers and schools, impact on teaching and department practice was by no means universal. Some schools or departments within schools dropped out of the project and abandoned the work mid-course. Others continued to participate, but completed assignments superficially, making little use of the feedback they had been given. Several schools encouraged the continued participation of interested *individual* teachers, but declined to implement the work among others. Participants were successful in only a few departments in engaging large numbers of colleagues in implementing common assessments, setting common performance standards, and using data to plan instructional improvements.

After two and a half years, WAC project staff described levels of activity or implementation in project schools/departments as shown in figure 2.

II. A LOOK INTO THE WORK OF THE HIGH SCHOOL INSTRUCTIONAL LEADERSHIP INITIATIVE

Collaborative Unit Planning and Standard Setting

WAC's efforts to support the implementation of standards-based instruction engaged teachers in a process of planning an instructional unit grounded in a performance standard. The process is referred to as "backward-mapping" because it unfolds from collaborative work to determine the precise nature of the work students are expected to do and proceeds from there to plan instructional experiences targeted to those expectations.*

Many participants are drawn to the work because backward-mapping makes intuitive sense. Although contrary to the ways in which teachers have been traditionally taught to plan lessons or units, it asserts that the instructional planning process should begin with the end in mind; that teachers should know what students are expected to know and do; and on what criteria their work will be judged. The lessons they plan are then targeted (and differentiated as necessary) to ensure that students are adequately prepared to perform at this level. Teachers tell us that, described in this way, the instructional planning process puts flesh on the bones of the call for "standards-based reform"—helping them to understand how this policy initiative should influence class-room practice.

This way of thinking about instruction has particular appeal to many high school teachers. At a time in their development when students have a great need for strong relationships with interested adults, this approach helps bring teachers and students together. Instead of leaving students in the dark about what the teacher wants, expectations are public. With explicit goals in sight, the teacher is viewed not as an obstacle to be overcome (e.g., *"I have to get through Mr. Smith's class"*), but as a support to students.

High school teachers often talk about the need for the students to take increasing responsibility for their own learning; and many rec-

---

*Although differing in some aspects, the process is similar to the work promoted by Grant Wiggins and Jay McTighe in *Understanding by Design*; and by the Education Trust in its project called *Standards in Practice*.

ognize that clear expectations, high quality assessment, and feedback provide the tools for students to do just that. In learning to articulate their expectations, implement rich assessments, and provide data to students, teachers foresee the opportunity to help students assess their own progress, articulate their strengths and weaknesses, and attend to those areas on which they need the most help.

Many high school teachers are drawn to the work by their awareness of the inequities in school experiences among students. Most acknowledge that some students are expected to do more than others, and that those students who are assumed to be unable or unready are often denied access to the kinds of learning experiences offered to their peers. These teachers recognize that the way they are trained and the conditions under which they work seldom allow them to come to agreements about what can be expected of all students. Some harbor resentment that other teachers expect too little of their students, and still others have become so isolated that they worry their own standards may be too low. The process of setting shared performance standards provides a forum to confront these issues.

For a great many teachers, this kind of collaborative work is attractive because it draws them into a professional community and provides opportunities for them to learn from and with colleagues. Teachers typically work in nearly total isolation from even those colleagues who teach the same grade or course. The collaborative unit development process facilitates the exchange of ideas and strategies among novice and more experienced teachers.

But despite the many motives that bring teachers to this work, few find it smooth going. Collaborative unit planning and analysis of student work serve as a Rorschach test of the knowledge, assumptions, values, and beliefs that drive instructional practice. Observations of groups at work sometimes revealed norms that made collaborative work difficult and challenge the goals of standards-based reform. The following are examples of this.

Beliefs that native ability rather than effective teaching and effort account for student performance: Despite the professional mantra "All kids can learn," teachers revealed their grave doubts that some students will ever achieve to high levels. Low-level assignments and simplistic assessments were based on the assumption that these were all a given group of students could do. Sometimes, student work was granted a satisfactory score because "the kid tried," whether or not the work met agreed-upon criteria. Teachers at times seemed disinterested in diagnosing confusion from the work students produced, because they had little intention of varying their instructional practices.

Resistance to the idea that teachers bear responsibility for creating credible evidence of what students are learning in their classrooms: Teachers were sometimes as reluctant to give an assessment designed by a colleague as they were a state test. "I don't teach this stuff in my class." "I know how my kids are doing. Why don't you just trust my analysis?" "I want kids to spend their time learning, not proving to others what they've learned." Fundamentally, some questioned whether teachers should assume responsibility for what students learned, especially at the high school level. Participants often had great difficulty articulating the criteria they applied to judgments of student performance and doubted that agreements could ever be reached among groups of teachers. Some advocated that teachers had no right to judge a student's work against any criterion other than what the student himself thought important.

Teachers who lack content and pedagogical knowledge of the subject areas they are teaching: In creating units of instruction, teachers often revealed their own lack of understanding of the subject matter. This lack of content or pedagogical expertise revealed itself in admissions by teachers that they did not know what a given content standard was referring to; in assessment tasks they created or selected that were unrelated to cognitive demands of the standard; in lessons or assignments that were a poor match to what students would be expected to know or do; or in the teachers' inability to analyze the skills required by an assessment task to plan an appropriate sequence of lessons to prepare for it.

Fierce protection of teacher autonomy: Even though they may have been drawn to this work by the goal of raising and coming to agreement about expectations for student performance, teachers were often reluctant to push colleagues to do anything that was not already part of their classroom routine. The topics of a given unit, the readings students would do to prepare for an assessment, and the agreement to administer a given assessment or use common grading standards generally were voluntary. Teachers sometimes spoke off the record about how they wished administrators would "make everyone do this," but when speaking openly, they defended the need for every teacher to decide for themselves what they would teach, what they would give students to do and how they would judge student work.

A reticence to question or challenge professional peers: The work revealed a strong compulsion to mask or bury disagreements among colleagues. Participants often seemed to have a vested interest in making it appear that there were few, if any, disagreements about what students should learn, the kinds of assignments or assessments they should be given, or how that work should be judged. Oftentimes, disagreements that did surface were settled quickly when one side gave in, rather than prolong the discussion. Even when concerns were revealed in private to project facilitators, seldom were they brought to light in discussions among peers. Often efforts to calibrate judgments of student performance among teachers or to check on the reliability of teachers' scores in relation to one another were dismissed as unnecessary. Sometimes teachers acquiesced publicly to decisions made by the group and then subverted those same decisions when it came time for implementation.

While each of these norms or beliefs could be observed in the work, they were also challenged by it. As participants worked together through a deliberately slow and detailed instructional planning process and took time at each step to become conscious about the criteria that play into design decisions, they were challenged to consider what those conversations revealed about what students are currently being taught, which students have access to what learning opportunities, and on what basis student work is currently being evaluated. They were encouraged to negotiate and internalize a shared understanding of what "high level" performance means and the kinds of work students must do if they are to achieve to high levels.

Few, if any, teachers came to the work with the expectation that it might cause them to reexamine what and how they teach; to question their beliefs about what students can and should be able to do; or to renegotiate their relationships with professional peers. Yet for many, this has been the most significant outcome of their participation. Participants leave the project with a unit that may serve as a useful classroom resource, but more significantly, some leave with ways of thinking about students, instructional planning, and professional relationships that will influence their work in the classroom and with colleagues on a daily basis.

Influencing Practice: Challenging Teachers' Expectations
for Student Performance

Typically, an individual teacher's expectations are shaped by her experience and beliefs. Living as they do in isolated classrooms, teachers cannot help but draw conclusions about what students can do by looking at what their own students do from year to year. The standards movement, on the other hand, asks teachers to consider what students might be able to do given access to a consistently high quality instructional program and progressively challenging experiences. The difference between what teachers are confident students can do; what they think "the state" demands; and what they *might like* to expect of their students creates a constant tension. But the collegial interaction, the sharing of expectations, feedback, and strategy can give participants the courage to think outside their own experience.

The math department in one project school told the story of how collaboration around a common assessment generated increased expectations for students. Guided only by the state content standards, the first draft of their assessment of the standard calling for students to "know, derive and solve problems involving the perimeter, circumference, area, volume, lateral area, and surface area of common geometric figures" provided students with a set of geometric figures for which the length of the sides were given. Students were asked to calculate the perimeter and area of these figures. A teacher from this department noted, "We gave that assessment, and we were really pleased with ourselves because the kids aced it."

But in the collaborative setting where department staff reviewed these data, the celebration did not last long. A number of teachers questioned the group's expectations. One teacher leader explained:

> We had to ask ourselves if that was what the state really meant for high school students. If you look at the standards, calculating perimeter and area shows up for the first time in fourth grade. So, we needed to figure out what the high school version of this standard is . . . otherwise we'd just go on teaching the same thing they were supposed to have learned in elementary school.

Acknowledging feedback from project facilitators and colleagues, the teachers revised their assessment to include problems in which students had to solve for unknowns—requiring application of their algebra skills within the geometry class. The teachers' challenge as they now describe it is to ensure that every teacher is armed with the instructional strategies necessary to support students to this level of performance.

Similarly, when teachers planned to include several multistep problems on the common math assessments, some teachers complained that these new tasks were too hard and lobbied that the tasks include directions that would guide the students through each step. But, another teacher challenged this position saying:

> I had to wonder. Do we really have to build in these steps and hold students' hands in that way . . . or do we just need to teach them and give them practice in doing lots of multistep problems?

Sometimes the conversation about how to score an assessment generates insights about expectations for student performance. Asked to do an initial impressionistic sorting of student work, math teachers from different schools found that the student work revealed only two distinct levels of performance: right and wrong.

> We didn't have any reason for anything but a two-point rubric, because we hadn't caused students to demonstrate any conceptual understanding of the problems we had given them. It made me wonder whether we had enough balance in our curriculum. Maybe we only expect kids to calculate, without knowing why they are doing it.

When participants come together to determine the characteristics of student work that will be deemed adequate in meeting the performance standard, more opportunities to strengthen the connection between expectations for student performance and the work of classroom teachers emerge. In yet another example, when reviewing student work requiring students to do a research paper, teachers were dismayed to find many papers in which students clearly had copied a good portion of the papers from other sources.

Several teachers noted that although the unit had a lesson teaching "steps in paraphrasing," it did not provide students practice in synthesizing ideas from several different sources and composing the ideas in their own words. Said one teacher, "We're constantly telling kids, 'Write this in your own words,' but do we really teach them how to do that?"

Teachers agreed to design and share lessons and exercises that taught students to synthesize ideas from various texts into their own words. In taking responsibility for their students' weaknesses, these teachers were refusing to compromise their beliefs about what was possible for students.

Influencing Practice: Connecting What Teachers Do to What Students Learn

So many factors influence a student's performance that teachers often lose sight of their own power to influence student learning through instruction. The unit development process helps participants see how targeted instruction can strengthen the bridge between what teachers do and what students produce.

The first step in the unit development process involves "unpacking" the standard(s) that serve as the foundation for the unit. The "unpacking" involves getting beyond simply the topic of the standard to understanding what level of cognitive challenge the standard implies. For example, the California content standards for English in ninth and tenth grades state that students should write persuasive compositions in which they "structure arguments in a sustained and logical fashion; and . . . address reader's concerns, counter claims, biases, and expectations." Working together, teachers analyze exactly what it will take to prepare students to do those things. In this case they recognized that students would necessarily have to know and be taught the following:

- to recognize a position statement and write one of their own
- to identify models and name criteria for "sustained" and "logical" writing and to identify those criteria in the writing of others as well as their own
- enough contextual information about the topic to identify common concerns, counter positions, or biases related to a given position

The "unpacking" conversation allows teachers to begin to surface their own confusion about the meaning of the standard(s), to begin to explore how the desired new skill fits with previous standards, and to learn from one another about critical connections within the content area. The conversation might generate awareness that if students are expected to write logical arguments, they will first need opportunities to read and analyze examples of arguments written by others. They might explore together what is meant by "sustained" or "logical"; discuss the kinds of writing errors that students typically make that interfere with their argument; or what examples of persuasive writing might be used as teaching models. At its best the discussion might motivate the sharing of lesson plans that have been used successfully.

Having unpacked the standard, teachers draft possible assessment tasks, think about the criteria students will need to meet in their response to that task, and then plan the instructional and practice opportunities that must be included in the unit. The department chair at one school reported that what at first seemed like an extremely tedious task translated into changes in the ways instruction was designed and structured.

> You just don't hear anybody say, "I have this great activity" anymore. They focus on the standards and what kind of instruction they'll need to provide. When our teachers assigned all students to do a research paper, they didn't just say to the kids, "do a paper." They broke it down to . . . the skills involved and then what they had to teach.

Teacher leaders from other schools commented about how the opportunity to practice aligning instructional opportunities to expectations for student performance affected their daily lesson planning and delivery:

> I have adjusted how I teach to build the student's ability to solve problems. I look at what they are required to know, and I break the lessons down in smaller increments. The student doesn't become so overwhelmed and if they follow through with me they experience greater success.

Influencing Practice: Developing a Professional Community around Technical Issues of Instruction

The work of ILI acknowledges that if you want to influence what and how students learn in high school, you need to influence how the faculty in departments work together. A recent long-term study of high schools illustrated the power of the professional community to influence teacher practice and attitudes. The study concluded that how and what teachers teach are influenced—for better or worse—by the nature of interactions those teachers have with colleagues who teach the same subject in their school. Some professional communities strengthen instructional practice while others protect the status quo. (McLaughlin and Talbert, 2001).

ILI gives rise to strong professional communities within departments in high schools by helping department leaders and their colleagues surface issues of student performance in terms of what is being taught, how it's evaluated, and what can be done to maximize student achievement. The goal is to develop both the instructional and leadership skills necessary to sustain what has been called a strong "technical culture"

(Johnson, 1990; Siskin, 1994), where teachers are drawn together not only by congeniality, but by a shared sense of responsibility for and efficacy about improving instruction.

Through the project, participants learn to use a set of heuristic devices and protocols for developing instructional units, negotiating performance standards, analyzing student work from common assessments, and planning action to address issues arising from their analysis of student performance. These tools guide the work of teachers as they learn skills themselves and then are used by teacher leaders in facilitating collaborative work within the department. The interactions the project aims for are not unlike those described as "Lesson Study"*— albeit, with primary focus on internalizing the characteristics of desired student performance and then planning targeted, explicit instruction to prepare students to complete work at the desired level.

English teachers in one department talked about how following the protocols for looking at student work involved more teachers and changed the conversation among them in important ways.

> We have a lot of people in our department who don't even feel the need to talk to others. They don't think they have much to learn. But the project gives us an objective process. It's about the unit and the student work, not individual people. (So) everyone has become a willing collaborator.

Describing a recent text adoption process, an English teacher-leader reported that project participation not only influenced the ability of her colleagues to be critical consumers of commercial materials, but helped the group to reach consensus on what can often be a divisive issue:

> Those of us who had developed units were much more careful about whether the text we were reviewing was really aligned to the standards, whether it had the right kind of opportunities to learn. The publishers all claim that their products are aligned, but we could see that they weren't all the same. When it came time to select, we all chose the same series.

The math department from one school chose to go beyond the project requirements and organized several entire courses around sets of

---

*The term "Lesson Study" describes collaborative work among teachers to plan, critique, and continuously revise and share lessons. First described to American teachers in the work of Harold Stevenson and James Hiebert who found this form of professional development to be common practice in Japanese schools, the practice is increasingly seen as professional development in U.S. schools. The ILI unit development process is similar to the planning portion of lesson study, but as currently conceived and implemented does not include observations of teaching practice.

common assessments. All teachers who taught these courses contributed to the design of the assessments and scoring guides. The department agreed that 80 percent of a student's grade would be based on these common assessments.

The strong professional community forged by the effort to build and agree on the assessments sends an important message to students: "When kids transfer from another teacher's class into mine, because they think I might be easier than the other guy, I just ask them for the assessments they've taken so far and tell them that those count for grades in my class just exactly as they do in the other teacher's class." Students learn that getting good grades may have more to do with effort than their luck in drawing an "easy" teacher.

When this same department carved out the time to do collaborative scoring of its assessments, teachers from throughout the department were involved whether or not they taught the course in which the assessment was given. Said one teacher: "Who has a bigger stake in whether kids are getting the right stuff in Algebra? It's the calculus teachers!" The cross-fertilization of course expertise allowed the group to explore questions such as "Will the work we are expecting of students in algebra prepare them for calculus? And, if not, what more do we need to prepare students to do?"

Another school's math department decided that to facilitate collaborative learning among teachers, every member of the department would, in the following year, teach at least one section of Algebra I. "Algebra is so important for the students, and we decided we needed everyone's expertise. Scoring common assessments was such a powerful learning experience for us that we decided this decision would generate more opportunities for common learning. If we're all teaching algebra, we can work together on this shared focus."

Influencing Practice: Developing a Sense of Personal
and Lateral Accountability

Critics of the trend toward top-down, external accountability mechanisms argue that they ignore the critical role of building internal accountability (Newman, King, and Rigdon, 1997; Elmore, 2002). By emphasizing the connection between what gets taught and what students learn, collaborative instructional unit planning and review of student work have the potential to renew teachers' sense of professional efficacy, along with helping them to accept greater responsibility for student learning. Project leaders from one school suggested that participation in this work influenced how teachers define successful teaching:

> I taught this lesson and judging by the questions kids were asking, I thought it really went well. I was really excited. And then I gave the assessment and more than half the kids didn't do very well. I had to admit I'd failed. (Math department chair)

When asked to think about how many of his own colleagues would be similarly willing to attribute poor student performance, at least in part, to what teachers do in the classroom, both this department chair and his counterpart in English reported with confidence that the numbers were growing.

Equally important is how teachers use this work to communicate expectations for professional practice. In the world of high-stakes, top-down school accountability, this work has the potential for teachers to develop a "lateral," or teacher-to-teacher accountability and provides opportunities for teachers to support one another to improve instruction and increase student learning.

Participating teachers from one math department found the "unpacking the standards" exercise so valuable in building a shared understanding of requisite content that they wanted to involve all members of their department. They developed a resource guide that unpacked critical math standards for key courses. The document detailed the knowledge required for each of the state content standards, the skills that might be considered prerequisite to each, and examples of problems. The document was a tool for building ownership of the standards across the department and helped to fill in gaps in pedagogical content knowledge. "This will always be a work in progress. I want people to put in their own examples. Eventually we need to expand it by showing where in the text or other resources these types of lessons and items can be found."

Assessments were often designed to communicate expectations not just to students, but to teachers. In one English department, teacher leaders developed a common assessment requiring juniors to produce an essay for a college application. Asked why they chose to require this as a schoolwide assessment, the teacher leaders answered that their goal was to ensure that teachers had all students write college admissions essays and attend to those students who needed the most help. "We needed to say that it was important that every kid who needs it, gets help on this."

Similarly, in one math department, one teacher's challenge to include problems requiring skills in solving quadratic equations earlier in the year caused some soul-searching among her colleagues.

> (She) pushed us to include quadratics earlier. We really didn't want to do it because it was inconvenient for us. But she was right, and she won us over, because we knew that if we put it on the assessment earlier, it would signal to teachers that they needed to get to it earlier so that kids had time to practice.

In working together, teachers learned to confront each other about the ways in which personal expectations or expertise affected student performance. These new norms for collaborative work were powerfully illustrated one day when a group of English teachers was discussing an assessment developed to test student understanding of some of the more technical aspects of doing and reporting on research. Four or five times during the session, one teacher, whose comments consistently revealed her own lack of understanding of the content and low expectations for student performance, was confronted politely, but ardently by a variety of colleagues. Finally, while the group was discussing the appropriate criteria to judge a student's ability to paraphrase text, this same teacher said, "We've just got to accept that high school kids have a natural tendency to plagiarize." One of her colleagues responded:

> What you are hearing here from (us) is that we don't believe that. Kids can learn what we teach them. They plagiarize because we haven't figured out the best way to help them. If even we are confused by or don't understand what we're asking the kids to do, then they surely won't be able to do it. It's our job to make sure that we know this stuff and learn to teach it so that our kids can do it. That's our responsibility!

III. THE CRITICAL ELEMENT: THE SYNERGY OF TEACHER AND ADMINISTRATIVE LEADERSHIP

Despite this work, many participants remained immune to its effects. Several reported seeing little opportunity for application of the process conducted in ILI workshops to their day-to-day practice. Still others appreciated the project's assistance in developing common assessments that could be given *to students*, but were less enthusiastic about the project's emphasis on using data from those assessments to examine teacher practice. Still others reported that they valued the work personally, but were unable to engage colleagues back at their sites.

Participants where the work seemed to have the greatest impact on instructional practices attributed that progress to supportive administrators. And not surprisingly, many individuals who valued the work, but did not see it take hold in their schools, held administrators, in part, responsible. Supportive administrators not only provided resources to pay for teachers' time, but signaled that collaborative unit planning and shared performance standards were not just the work of project participants but were an expectation for the whole department or school. The principal from one school not only participated in collaborative work sessions, but provided teacher-leaders with formal "coaching training" to help them support their colleagues. In another school, district office leaders attended collaborative teacher work sessions and drew on the work to influence other schools.

While research acknowledges the critical role administrators play, the importance of *teacher leadership* is often overlooked. Teachers in formal leadership roles as well as many unannointed leaders wielded great power to determine the project's reach and its influence on instructional practice. Teachers take responsibility for the effort at their own schools in several ways:

- facilitating the work of collaborative groups to maximize teacher learning within and across course assignments
- tacitly acknowledging the unevenness of content and pedagogical knowledge within the department
- recognizing the skills required of collaborative work while encouraging and modeling their use
- questioning their own expectations for students and those of their peers
- modeling both humility and a sense of efficacy

At nearly every turn of collaborative unit planning, a choice needed to be made whether to carry out the development process simply to complete the unit or for the opportunity it provided for collaborative learning. Teacher leaders facilitated the project's work with attention to maximizing teacher learning. While they could have more easily met project deadlines by completing the work alone or in pairs, they used the project's protocols to engage their colleagues in discussions to negotiate performance criteria and then to engage in collaborative scoring and analysis of the resulting data. Some cajoled the whole department to participate in the dialogue, and they facilitated conversations about how the findings might influence work in other courses.

Even when collaborative work time was not available, some teacher leaders found ways to facilitate dialogue. In one math department, the department chair served as the hub of ongoing virtual collaboration among colleagues. Assessments were drafted by individuals or small groups of teachers and submitted to the chair for review. She then submitted the draft to colleagues for critique and incorporated their feedback. But she recognized that the goal was not just to get an assessment that everyone would agree to, but one that reflected rigorous standards and guided teachers to improve instructional practice. "Sometimes I really have to push on them. Sometimes someone will suggest items for the test that have nothing to do with the standard, and I'll have to ask 'What's this doing here?' And they'll tell me they put it there because it's easy, and they taught it. I can't let that happen."

Effective teacher leaders took upon themselves the responsibility for the logistics that made it possible for others to learn together. They planned and facilitated meeting agendas, strategically selected and prepared multiple copies of assessments or student work to be reviewed, and typed and circulated the results of collaborative work. While each of these leaders would have welcomed additional clerical help, they also recognized that their expertise and leadership played a critical role in promoting collaborative learning. While describing the department-wide process of developing, circulating, revising, and cataloguing common assessments, the math department chair reflected:

> Sometimes when I'm typing up these assessments and getting them out to teachers, I think I'm just doing a big clerical task, and then I realize that it's important that I digest all the feedback I get, incorporate it into the assessment so that it represents the mathematics standards correctly, and then meet with colleagues so they understand why the assessment looks the way it does.

Although they were reluctant so say so publicly, these leaders acknowledged in various ways that teacher expectations and expertise within the department varied and that the work could be designed to maximize opportunities for teachers to learn from one another. They planned work groups so that more knowledgeable teachers would influence others, or so that teachers who had not been exposed to high-quality student work could do so and talk with the teachers in whose class it was produced. They took responsibility for circulating high-quality examples and resources to all colleagues, so that everyone had the opportunity to learn from them.

Teacher leaders who are instrumental in guiding the work to affect instructional practice acknowledge that teachers are required to relate to each other in new ways. These leaders are sensitive to the fact that they are asking their colleagues not only to expose their practice to the scrutiny of others, but also to make agreements to work collectively in the interest of improved performance. Recognizing that the skills required of these professional collaborations may be foreign to many teachers, these teacher leaders found ways to model and promote them. In one department teachers reviewed collaboration skills at the start of each meeting, identified those they most needed to work on, and then made time at the end of each meeting to critique the effectiveness of their work together.

At the same time these teacher leaders promoted collaborative work, they also took steps to address provocative issues. They made room for the voices of colleagues who pushed on established practices and stretched the comfort zone of their colleagues. They found ways to make threatening experiences acceptable, such as when they asked their colleagues to look at their student assessment data disaggregated by teacher. Teachers agreed to code the data so individuals could recognize their own scores, but not the scores of other teachers.

Teacher leaders took it upon themselves to stretch expectations for student performance, not just by saying they could be higher, but by making the connection between what students might do and what and how teachers teach. They paid attention to the cognitive challenge in the task(s) students were given, as well as whether students received adequate and well-targeted opportunities to learn. Their pushing often came in the form of a question rather than a direct challenge; their inquiry modeled both humility ("I wonder what would happen if we . . .") and the firm belief that instruction could significantly influence student performance.

Leaders in emerging professional cultures opted for the courageous conversation, even when compliance would suffice. Knowing that they would be demanding time from colleagues who had precious little of it, and knowing that the conversations they might generate could be messy, these leaders used their time to provoke dialogue and learning. In doing so, they received kudos from their colleagues:

> This is one of the most cohesive departments I've ever worked in, and I've worked in many. People like working here because there is so much collegial, professional support.

> We need more of this kind of conversation, where we look at the (student) work together and talk about what we think is good. I

especially appreciate my colleagues who developed and taught the
unit for making this happen.

But just as teacher leadership was the catalyst for learning in some
schools, it was a roadblock in others. In one school the department
chair felt so strongly that teachers should not be involved in this kind of
work unless they were paid above their base salary that he was able to
influence administrators to stop even voluntary efforts. In another, the
work done by teacher leaders in the project was rejected by colleagues
at the school:

> We were taught in ILI to develop instruction based on the standards.
> What the project taught really made sense to us. But some of our
> colleagues wanted us to develop units that were only related to the
> standards . . . Basically they wanted to do the literature they were
> always doing and not have to make any changes.

This same teacher speculated that it was this response from his colleagues that soured administrators' support for the work.

An enthusiastic project participant from another school recognized
that neither teachers nor administrators from his school had planned
adequately for readying others to take on collaborative instructional
planning:

> When I look at developing lesson plan capacity, I believe that our
> district now has several teachers who could write a lesson plan using
> backward mapping. Where we may have missed the mark is that we
> did not install an ongoing process that will continue to develop such
> plans. Unfortunately, I believe that we did not think the problem all the
> way through. Without a total buy-in from all the teachers and ongoing
> support to continue the process, we may fall far short of our intended
> outcome. Leadership must come from the rank and file. This is our
> Achilles' heel.

Teacher leaders who pushed the work in ways that influenced
department-wide instructional practice were able to take those risks
because they knew their administrators encouraged them to do so.
Furthermore, if these same courageous teacher leaders were to sustain
their efforts and go deeper, they would need additional support. Several
of them worried about just how far they could continue to push their
colleagues; what their authority was to do so; and whether they had
the expertise or time necessary to support deeper levels of collaborative
learning.

But there were also schools with supportive administrators, where the work remained superficial at best. Administrative leadership is a necessary but insufficient resource in the effort to improve instructional practice in high schools. Teacher leadership was critical to the rigor and depth of the collaborative unit planning process and these conversations' impact on classroom practice. It was sometimes teacher leaders who stood in the first line of defense against the implementation of standards-based instructional practices. And, likewise, it was teachers, often working collectively, whose leadership kept debilitating beliefs, traditional norms, and common misconceptions from holding sway.

IV. IMPLICATIONS FOR ONGOING WORK

The Instructional Leadership Initiative seeks, at a minimum, to institute a set of common curriculum-embedded assessments and performance standards. With greater investment in the work, schools can learn to use the assessments to focus professional conversations around issues of what is being taught, which students have access to what kinds of opportunities to learn, and how student work is and should be evaluated. And when these conversations permeate the professional culture, we may begin to see influences in department-wide practices and classroom teaching on a daily basis.

Within ILI, it was possible to see both the worst and the best of these kinds of efforts. On one extreme were individuals and departments that went through the motions of collaborative unit development, but saw in it little application to their everyday work. On the other extreme, multiple departments used the work to build a professional community and focus the school on instructional issues that affect student learning. While administrative leadership at the school either blocked or paved the way for growth in the professional community among teachers, teacher leadership played the most critical role in how deeply the work influenced instructional practice. Teachers in both formal and informal leadership roles maximized learning opportunities for colleagues and set the expectation that teachers would reexamine current practice in light of these shared learning experiences.

For those of us moving forward with work similar to the Instructional Leadership Initiative, here are some important considerations:

Schools should engage in the work of building common assessments and performance standards only if they have already begun to envision how those tools will be embedded in a system that promotes teacher learning and collective action. Coming to consensus on an assessment and performance standard that reflects good instructional practice is messy work. Although the process can be valuable for those teachers involved, (Falk, 2000; Jamentz, 1996), that value does not extend to colleagues charged only with administering the product of that effort and reporting the scores. For those teachers, the assessment serves as little more than another test. The influence on instruction happens primarily when teachers engage in dialogue about how the assessment and the results affect classroom practice. And the influence is sustained only when decisions and new learning become expectations for department-wide practice. In several ILI schools, participants or administrators were unwilling to invest necessary resources or feared the ensuing conversation. By contrast, in ILI schools making greatest use of the work, resources were invested in ensuring broad participation at the school, and the implicit message from administrative and teacher leaders was that everyone was expected to be involved in these opportunities for collaborative work.

As school leaders continue to invest in this work, they should ensure that the school plan includes the necessary commitment of resources not only for initial development of assessments or units, but for their ongoing use as catalysts for professional learning. The school plans should reflect the expectation that all teachers will use the assessments or units, and include accountability measures for teachers and administrators.

A great deal of classroom time is already devoted to test taking. If the units and assessments developed in projects like ILI will not be designed and used in ways that are value-added to teacher learning, they are probably not worth the effort.

No school should engage in this work without opportunities for external review and feedback of their work. ILI was designed to break down isolation among teachers within a department and to expose teachers in participating schools to the work of other schools and feedback from external content reviews. The design acknowledged that to influence teachers' learning, as well as their expectations for student performance, we needed to design the professional development opportunity in ways that gave teachers access to expertise outside their daily experience. Teacher isolation makes feedback both rare and essential.

Many participating teachers valued these opportunities to hear from others outside their communities, and several mentioned that access to the thinking of teachers from other schools or from content experts caused them to question their own expectations for students. For many, attention to the feedback offered in external reviews made the difference between units judged to be "to standard" or "not yet to standard."

External review and feedback were also important in helping the schools make sense of their efforts in relation to more formal state accountability systems. For some, the intent was to develop curriculum-embedded assessments that would help teachers understand what students needed to be better prepared for high-stakes tests; and for others the intent was to implement a set of assessments that provided evidence of the knowledge and skills these large-scale assessments were unable to capture. To succeed, locally developed assessments and performance standards should be reviewed in relation to what is expected on larger scale measures.

The exercise of reviewing locally developed work against external expectations may, on the one hand, validate the schools' efforts, and on the other, create fodder for school and teacher leaders to reexamine their expectations and practices. As schools plan to continue common assessment and unit development, they should build in multiple opportunities for review and feedback from outside the immediate school community.

The interdependence of administrator and teacher leadership must be acknowledged and nurtured. Administrators encourage the development of strong professional communities focused on instruction, and teacher leaders make them work. The kinds of teacher leadership on display in some ILI schools take both courage and skill. Their work required group facilitation, negotiations, and problem-solving skills, as well as strong pedagogical content knowledge in their subject areas. Schools well on their way to building strong professional communities focused on instructional improvement, funded release time or clerical support for teacher leaders to plan project-related meetings, and one school offered specific training in coaching. Administrators occasionally attended work-group meetings not only to signal their support, but to model collaborative behaviors and set an expectation through their modeling that everyone should contribute productively.

In schools with emerging professional cultures focused on instruction, administrators set the tone. The focus on instructional improvement was evidenced not only by their support of ILI work, but by other investments in professional development focused on classroom practice. Administrators and teacher leaders spent time in classrooms and could talk about what they saw in relation to the goals of the project and the school. Asked how they first came to be involved in the ILI, one department chair told a story about her principal:

> She came to our staff meeting, and she told us that nothing was going to
> get any better for kids in this school unless we did something to change
> what we were doing in the classroom. We were pretty angry when we
> heard that, and lots of people said, "Who does she think she is, telling
> us that?" But now most people think that she was probably right. She is
> constantly asking us to think about instruction, and she expects us to
> work on it.

This principal was respected for her willingness to acknowledge
the complexities of effective instruction, for her tenacity in pushing
teachers to focus their attention there, and for her willingness to invest
in instructional improvement in various ways. She recognized that it
would take teachers with pedagogical and content expertise and the
leadership skills to build professional learning communities powerful
enough to influence classroom practice.

Adequate investments need to be made in building teacher leadership
skills and resources set aside to help key teacher leaders plan for and
follow through with their leadership responsibilities. Administrators
should be able to communicate to the communities outside the school
about the purpose of this work and how it connects to other instructional improvement efforts.

When schools invest in teachers' collaborative instructional planning,
negotiations to establish performance standards, and analysis of student work, the potential payoffs extend far beyond the unit they create.
Encouraged by administrators, and pushed by colleagues, participants
in this kind of collaborative effort may begin to rethink their expectations for students, for their own work, and professional relationships.
But in high schools that have yet to invest in the kind of administrative
and teacher leadership required, these same efforts run the risk of giving
credence to, and helping to perpetuate, the very beliefs and practices
that stand in the way of effective standards-based instruction.

❖ ❖ ❖

Commentary

MICHELLE KALINA

Kate Jamentz describes an exciting and productive approach to professional teacher development that has the potential to change prac-

tice resulting in better student learning aligned to agreed-upon state standards. The processes she describes in the Instructional Leadership Initiative give faculty the opportunity to develop collaborative skills that allow them to have important conversations about what is taught, how it is taught, how it is assessed, and the rubrics (grading guides) to assess the student work.

Although these may be groundbreaking approaches to the teaching/learning process, the public's response might be a big "Duh." Isn't that what teachers are supposed to do? So perhaps one of the most provocative results of this work is that it speaks to the need to reflect on what is happening in schools of education and why this approach to learning/teaching methodology is not reflected in the curricula. Why aren't teachers prepared to work collaboratively, and why does the old paradigm still prevail at most schools? Why is teaching still being done behind closed doors, and why are so many teachers still clinging to the notion of "academic freedom" as their defense to do so?

If schools of education are preparing future teachers to participate in a professional, collaborative community, then what is happening as they enter the teaching environment? Why is there such a gap between theory and practice? While ILI is successful with some of the teacher-leaders it works with, it is not successful in every situation. How to make such an approach to professional communities and good instructional practice a more universal occurrence is the question left for practitioners to unravel. Here is a model that works well with faculty and administrators and has a positive effect on classroom instruction; yet, it fails or works poorly in some settings. We need to do more with this and other models that foster conversations among faculty that lead to better student outcomes.

A second area of comment is how does this type of practice inform classroom teachers' understanding of the metacognitive skills students use when engaged in collaborative/cooperative work in the classroom? Jamentz states numerous times in the piece that the methodology used brings teachers and students together in a partnership focused on student learning. How then do the participants in the ILI training focus on their own process as learners? Do they maintain a "learning log" capturing their observations about the collaborative process they are using to deconstruct standards, develop appropriate and rigorous criteria and assessments, and build classroom practices and activities to support and achieve the outcomes? What reflective activities are used with teachers to surface their questions and concerns about the lesson and assessment development process? Are the various models of collaborative/cooperative learning used with teachers so that they might have several models to choose from in designing their own instruction?

This case study highlights, in an indirect way, the need to align the curricula of schools of education with the changing focus of research and practice. Perhaps what Jamentz speaks to is a new paradigm for training teachers—one focused on hands-on practice and reflection on the outcomes of the teaching. The "rubber meets the road" in the classroom environment, and teachers, both new and seasoned, need the opportunity to try new ways of operating within a "safe environment" and then have the opportunity to reflect and share those reflections with other practitioners.

Research on this subject suggests that faculty value the opportunity to share with their colleagues what is happening in their classrooms and to receive feedback about the possible meaning and future actions the faculty member may take. Japanese teachers often participate in faculty professional learning communities where they have ongoing opportunities to discuss teaching questions that emerge as outcomes of practice, and they gain insight into both their own practices and exposure to new ways of facilitating learning.

The California Partnership for Achieving Student Success (Cal-PASS) brings teams of faculty together by discipline on a monthly basis to look at data about student success within a region and then discuss the degree of misalignment that exists across segments and ways to improve alignment and student learning. Faculty report that the monthly council meetings are some of the most valued professional conversations they have in terms of their own development as faculty. In addition, they report that by using a Classroom Assessment Technique (CAT) model, they are learning more about themselves as teachers and using the knowledge to change their practices (Cal-PASS internal documents, 2005–2007).

Similarly, faculty trained in CAT's methodology in the 1990s met once a month to review their experiences using the CAT model in their classrooms. Participating faculty reported that the most valuable part of the training process was the opportunity to talk with their peers about what was going on in their classrooms and receive feedback.

The California Academic Partnership Program brings its grant participants together multiple times during the grant period to share their work with others, creating an opportunity to talk in both structured and unstructured conversations, thus facilitating the professional networks that are so critical to sustain the work. The participants also

report that the opportunity to work with their colleagues collaboratively and learn from one another is what most informs their teaching
practice and results in better student performance.

A positive next step, building on the work of Jamentz and others,
would be to create teacher training models where teachers collaboratively develop lessons and assessments, instead of planning in isolation. During and after the teaching, teachers note their observations
in reflective logs or annotate the lessons, and they then share these
reflections and annotations with other teachers. The collective conversations would form the basis for revisions and adjustments to improve
instruction. If this collaborative model were introduced in preservice
programs, then planning together and building instructional teams
would more likely be the norm rather than the exception in schools.

The ILI model demonstrates the efficacy of faculty working collaboratively with each other to create more productive learning environments. In so doing, Jamentz provides faculty with the opportunity to
have a structured conversation related to practice and perhaps makes
them more aware of their own learning process. The ILI model also
provides a viable pedagogy for training teachers as well.

❖ ❖ ❖

Commentary

LORIE ROTH

A pervasive assumption about P-18 (preshool–graduate school) relations
is that ideas and innovations percolate downward in the academic hier-
archy. The common understanding seems to be that doctoral programs
in education produce research findings; these findings are disseminated
to teacher education faculty, who, in turn, transmit good research-
based practice to undergraduates who will become K-12 teachers.

In short, it is assumed that creativity and innovation trickle down
from doctoral universities to teacher education programs to high school
teachers.

What we learn from Kate Jamentz, however, is that instead of perco-
lating down, fresh ideas are bubbling up. The High School Instructional
Leadership Initiative (ILI) is a radical departure from standard class-

room practice, and not only are the concepts and actions promulgated by ILI having an effect on grades 8–12, they are also affecting the way that college and university faculty think and behave.

When I was a faculty member at a university, I chose the books I wanted to teach, I decided what main points I wanted to emphasize, I decided what tests I would give, and I decided what grades students would receive. I almost never talked to my colleagues about what I was teaching and how I was grading, and it never occurred to me that I should. I was fully socialized into a system in which individual faculty had total control over subject matter, methods of assessment, and student grades. Despite the fact that my colleague across the hall was teaching the same course that I was, I never talked to her about subject matter, textbooks, tests, required papers, and criteria for grades. My classroom was my kingdom, and her classroom was her kingdom.

That's the way it was supposed to be, right? And, if at the end of a semester, my class's overall GPA was 2.0 and her class's was 3.5, well, she must have been an easy grader, I supposed, while I, on the other hand, upheld high standards. I, unlike some others, knew how to separate the wheat from the chaff.

As a tenured professor, the qualities that mattered most to me were independence, autonomy, self-reliance, and individuality. Frankly, I was interested in what *I* wanted to teach. It really never occurred to me that I should, perhaps, think about what students needed to learn.

The traditional culture of university teaching and high school teaching into which I was socialized—along with millions of others—has been challenged by Kate Jamentz and her colleagues at the Western Assessment Collaborative (WAC) at WestEd. Her article on the ILI describes a revolutionary approach to teaching and learning, and as in the case of most revolutions, some citizens cling even more fervently to the status quo, while others find the new order to be transformative and liberating.

For many high school teachers participating in the ILI, this was not just another professional development workshop; it was a life-changing experience. The ILI process, which was promulgated in the WAC workshops, required teachers from the same discipline (especially mathematics and language arts) to undertake a process for ensuring that students learn. The process includes these steps:

- Identify a standard to master—and understand its constituent parts
- Create a common assessment of the standard

- Create and teach an instructional unit that will ensure that students meet the standard
- Administer the assessment and develop a shared performance standard
- Analyze data to see what actions might be needed

In undertaking ILI, Jamentz and colleagues challenged participants to confront at least some of the traditional dichotomies:

Independence vs. collaboration—Teachers had to work as a group. As a group they had to design an assessment. They had to agree upon a criterion that would signal mastery of a standard.

Implicit vs. explicit—Teachers had to verbalize their expectations of students.

Private vs. public—Teachers had to subject their teaching plans and assessment to peer review; that is, external reviewers commented on and evaluated the work that the teachers had done.

Many who participated in the ILI experience were converted to the process. However, maintaining the heightened experience proved to be more difficult when the participants returned to their home schools. The pressures and customs of traditional high schools made it easy to lapse from collaborative activities to individual ones.

Interestingly, it would appear that these innovations in high school instruction are starting to gain currency and respect in college classrooms. The assessment of student learning is starting to take root in higher education. Faculty are identifying learning outcomes and collaborating on assessments to improve student learning. Finally, after decades of teaching in isolation, university faculty have begun to implement the tenets promoted by ILI: collaboration and public statements of expectations for students. How strong and sustained will be the embrace of college faculty for these innovations? No one yet knows.

Expect Success

Interventions Beyond Remediation

KATRINE CZAJKOWSKI

ONE VISIONARY TEACHER LEADER can make a difference. Katrine Czajkowski shows us how. She initiated a Tutoring and Homework Center for mathematics, emulated by several other CAPP schools. This year the school began a Writing Center for English language arts tutoring. She also describes the department's process to develop common mathematics assessments, the Grade Recovery Program, and Summer Acceleration Classes. These four initiatives are built on the positive, but unusual notion of expecting success of students, rather than anticipating failure.

❖ ❖ ❖

In 1991, having just finished my first year working in a high school two miles from the U.S./Mexico Border, I wrote a hostile letter to the university where I received my secondary teaching credential. I expressed that I felt totally unprepared to work in a school serving marginalized students of color. I could hardly pronounce my students' last names, much less match instructional strategies to their educational experiences or cultural backgrounds. I had earned my bachelor's degree from a first-tier, East Coast university and found myself in Southern California, adrift on an educational sea without map, lifeboat, or oars. More disturbing than my personal angst was the way students were placed in the care of someone like me, a person "highly qualified" to teach them mathematics and English. Now, 15 years later, I see that first year in perspective: teaching, especially in diverse communities, is complicated business. Much is said about how hard it is to teach in tough schools; less is said about how hard it must be to be a student there.

Good teachers prosper when their students learn; good schools are places with a critical mass of good teachers. Good teaching does not fall from the sky. Rather, it is like a tree that needs frequent tending, water, and access to light through the canopy of what can be a suffocating jungle overhead. What follows are programs and services that hold both students and teachers accountable to the high expectations required for mutual success and to support student learning. The central tenet that schools can and must win in their struggle to advance opportunity to all members of American society guides these programs.

CONTEXT

The California Academic Partnership Program (CAPP) provides grants linking secondary schools with higher education institutions. The schools described here received two major CAPP grants; the first grant's goal was to increase the percentage of students attending four-year universities by increasing the number of students enrolling and succeeding in challenging college-prep courses. The second grant sought to increase students' performance on the California High School Exit Exam (CAHSEE) and increase students' success in the "A-G" courses required for admission to the California State University (CSU) and University of California (UC) systems. This project focused on teachers collecting, analyzing, and using data to improve classroom instruction. The grants funded the activities of a partnership of schools, the "Standards Mastery and Responsive Teaching" project, that became known as the "SMART" schools (see Table 2).

Chula Vista High School (CVH), home to approximately 2700 students, is located about five miles north of the U.S./Mexico border. Built in 1950, the school was designed for about 1500 students. Today about 80% of its students are of Latino descent, and 8% are African American. The rest of the students are mostly of Anglo and Pacific Islander backgrounds. Almost 70% of the students qualify for free or reduced-priced lunches. CVH's only magnet program is the School for the Creative and Performing Arts, which draws about 800, mostly

SMART SCHOOLS

Years	Schools	Major goal of grant	Focus of project
1995– 1999	Mar Vista High School Mar Vista Middle School UC, San Diego Southwestern College	Increase college-going rate	Support students' academic language proficiency in mathematics
2000– 2004	Mar Vista High School Chula Vista High School Chula Vista Middle School San Diego State University Southwestern College	Improve first-time CAHSEE pass rate; improve overall CAHSEE pass rate; increase enrollment in "A-G" college preparation courses	Help teachers collect, analyze, and use a variety of data to improve classroom practice

Anglo, students from throughout the Sweetwater Union High School District (SUHSD).

Mar Vista High (MVH) School serves similar students with a few key exceptions. While about a quarter of students at both CVH and MVH are identified English learners (ELs), more of the English learners at CVH are recent immigrants. Most of the ELs at MVH have been enrolled in public schools and tracked into bilingual courses for at least two years. Both CVH and MVH are located near large military bases, but MVH has more Anglo students (almost 15%) than CVH. CVH has one of the largest populations of African American students among SUHSD schools; these students achieve at a markedly lower level at both CVH and MVH than their Anglo and Latino peers. Overall, fewer than 30% of all graduates from MVH and CVH gain admission to four-year colleges or universities, and fewer than 25% actually enroll.

FUNDING

CAPP's grants at these partnership schools had specific goals and focused implementation plans. However, working with other CAPP-funded projects throughout California revealed early that each funded project pursued its goals in unique ways. These differences were partially due to variation among schools' cultures and financial priorities. However, CAPP-funded schools were all eligible for Title I and Title VII funding and had access to supplemental state and federal funds because of generally low performance by students with demonstrated need. Many of these schools received significant additional funding (over $100,000 per year) through the Immediate Intervention/ Underperforming Schools Program (II/USP). Without question, these schools benefited from having access to substantial additional funding that could support innovation on behalf of marginalized students.

However, what became clear through discussions among leaders of CAPP projects at various sites was that this money was not focused on clearly articulated, coherent, limited goals. Additionally, most of this money (amounting to over $2 million for one school) was directed at interventions grounded in an "acceptable loss" mentality. As schools are rife with the "education as war" metaphor, marginalized students— who comprised the majority at most of these partnership schools—were almost doomed to become casualties or "acceptable losses." SMART schools, like most California comprehensive high schools, pursue the mission of preparing *all* students for success in four-year universities. Yet few vocational programs remain, and magnet programs, like the School for Creative and Performing Arts at CVH, serve white students in overrepresented proportions. When fewer than one in four graduates actually attends a four-year college after graduation, the question looms large: what happens to the other 75%?

That such a low percentage of college-going graduates is accepted as the norm suggests that only minimal upward change in these numbers is expected, much less possible. The status quo drives everything in underachieving schools. Students are "placed" in specialized programs to fill capacity. Funding for supplemental programs follows predictable patterns. The district office sets up annual budgets using the previous year's distribution by expense category, making even minor program or personnel changes difficult and complicated by red tape. Seldom, if ever, are financial and human resources allocated based on a whole-scale rethinking of the educational program for marginalized students.

In 1999, when I learned that CVH would receive over $600,000 a year in Title I funding, I was tempted by the possibility of building a supplemental services program from scratch. Here was an opportunity to start anew, to spend money in what I thought might be the right way. As the "Categorical Coordinator" and full-time resource teacher responsible for designing, implementing, and monitoring these programs, I worked closely with a very supportive principal. He was perhaps the only person who could convince me to leave my students, along with coaching (aquatics and cross country) and club advising, those cocurricular activities that matter so much to students and adults who care about them. With his help, I was responsible for developing the school's annual Site Plan. I had authority to hire non-certificated staff, including tutors, instructional assistants, and clerks. I worked with parents and staff members to arrange enrichment classes and professional development institutes for teachers. In this encouraging environment, I was allowed to innovate in collaboration with diverse people around me.

GUIDING PRINCIPLES

While few schools have such an opportunity to "start over," I have worked with people from similar schools to reform ways to spend supplemental funding. I learned that it is possible to make money go much further if people apply some basic guidelines. Underlying these guidelines is a shared philosophy that students and their families can contribute a great deal more to schools than our system has traditionally expected. Once that expectation is clear, so is the mission: make the dreams a reality and challenge what stands in the way.

SMART schools, therefore, based the planning and implementation of their supplemental and core programs on two essential premises:

- Programs and services must *expect success first*, making potential failure a secondary concern
- All funding at sites must be viewed as a set of matching funds supporting achievement of a few key objectives, just as the mandated, but often peripheral School Site Plan suggests

The following are the critical guiding principles supporting these two premises:

- *Hold everybody accountable for services to students.* Publish records of meetings. Make budgets transparent. Provide broad access to data and information
- *Understand that tracking is a formula for disaster.* Accept the risky, but ethical position, of not labeling students
- *Nurture creativity* and *resourcefulness*, encouraging voices that challenge the status quo to be heard
- Base development of programs and services on the fundamental goal of *expanding equity and access to opportunity* for all students

- *Relish challenge and set high expectations* for every member of the educational community and use a culture of collaboration to maximize the effort
- *Consider teachers to be professionals and leaders.* Understand that teachers are motivated by their students' success
- *Acknowledge and engage the cultural context* in which education takes place

MAKING IT HAPPEN

One of the requirements of CAPP funding was regular networking among projects. Twice each year, teams of teachers, administrators, counselors, and district office staff from each CAPP project convened at a statewide conference. Exchanging ideas with the leaders of other CAPP-funded projects over the course of almost ten years helped us determine which of our SMART project activities had the greatest potential of dissemination beyond our project schools.

While the spirit of *No Child Left Behind's* "research-based" intervention guidelines deserves acknowledgement, they fail to recognize that schools are complex places where a causal relationship between intervention X and performance indicator Y is often difficult to establish reliably. Schools like those connected by SMART receive supplemental money for good reasons. They are challenging places to work and to learn. Having hope in the face of despair is often as good an indicator of progress as anything. Are new, qualified teachers coming to these schools? Are they staying? Do students participate in programs and services that require them to invest time and energy in school beyond the bell? Do teachers, both experienced and novice, make time during summers and weekends to improve their content and pedagogical knowledge? What kinds of new efforts are launched? What kinds of risks are members of the school community willing to take on behalf of students?

Answers to those questions are, for practitioners, more practical indicators of progress than students' national percentile rankings on nationally normed tests. They are measures of progress that provide formative data regarding how schools are working to ratchet up the level at which students, teachers, and administrators are expected to perform. Having served as Categorical Coordinator at CVH, I appreciate the importance of using quantitative measures for accountability. However, education is as much a process as a series of products recorded in the accountability ledger. In fact, it is the "process" of public education that makes enduring its slings and arrows worthwhile.

The efforts of the SMART schools have resulted in some hallmark programs and projects that have advanced student learning, improved our teaching, and sharpened our attention to curriculum, assessment, and accountability.

Math Tutoring and Homework Center

Open Monday through Thursday from 2:30 p.m. to 6:30 p.m., the Homework Center (HWC) is staffed by one to two certificated math teachers, one or two college students (math or science majors, most bilingual in Spanish and English), and two to three high school calculus tutors. Students work in groups; if they study for at least 30 minutes, they receive a HWC slip to present to their teachers or parents. College student tutors who work in the HWC are also assigned hours in classrooms during the school day so they are familiar with students' "reality" in various classrooms. A 10% sample of HWC students revealed that average geometry grades increased more than one whole letter grade over comparable non-HWC-attending geometry students. A schoolwide survey revealed the vast majority of HWC attendees visit "to get help" and not to receive extra credit, and the person providing the most critical help was a college student tutor.

Perhaps the most important characteristic differentiating the SMART HWC from other after-school tutorials is the expectation that students want to improve their performance in math. The HWC serves no punitive or disciplinary function, and students cannot be assigned to go there. Early in the implementation of both HWCs, I had to explain to teachers that "No, you cannot tell a student to 'serve tardies' or detention in the HWC. Yes, students can leave when they are done with their work. As long as they show evidence of learning, they can receive verification of attendance. It's not about seat time." Additionally, results of a student survey revealed that students with self-reported math grades of "D" attended the HWC more frequently than students with self-reported grades of "A" or "B." Confronted with this information, teachers could less easily claim that students "didn't care" about low grades. When teachers shared shifts in the HWC, they got to know their students more individually, building relationships that transferred to the classroom. The HWC was expected to be a "positive place," where students could work in groups and talk about learning. It beckoned students with the expectation of positive challenge and the support of qualified and caring people. Students could rely on school offering them an environment in which voluntary learning was, in fact, fun and challenging. Perhaps the flame of academic dreams could burn in its sheltering space.

We developed some specific guidelines for building a successful homework center.

Never cancel the center or change the schedule during a given semester. HWC support services are ongoing, consistent, and excellent. We initially offered services between 2:30 p.m. and 8:00 p.m. Monday through Thursday, but during the second semester we shortened the hours to end at 6:30 p.m. when we determined that we did not have a critical mass of students later in the evening. While supervised and run by teachers, the HWC has unconditional administrative support, especially in the rare event that emergencies pull teachers from their regularly scheduled shift, and administrative supervision is required.

Use a central academic location, such as the school library, with easy access by parents and others who seek contact with students or staff. Access to computers, books, and other resources is desirable. Using the cafeteria should be avoided. Students need to experience the positive intellectual "hum" of inquiry. You should court the librarian and promise accountability, following up promptly whenever any damage or loss occurs, and involving her or him in decisions regarding staffing and procedures.

Furnish the room with large tables and chairs, not traditional school desks. Students must learn to work collaboratively with tutors and with each other.

Expect students to need help with mathematics. You can verify this need by adding questions to annual schoolwide student surveys that ask students to identify the subject with which they need most help, what kinds of help they would like, and at what times.

Hire only mathematics-proficient tutors and teachers, regardless of other attributes. You should provide students with access to at least one certificated math teacher at all times. This individual also serves a supervisory role, but NEVER hire "just anybody" who is willing to do extra-duty time. Recent graduates of neighborhood schools who are currently studying math or science at local community colleges and universities are good choices, as are bilingual/bicultural people. You should give them as many work hours as you can, considering their college course schedules. Once I had a "critical mass" of these talented individuals, they referred me to friends and other highly qualified classmates. Most of the tutors were from the community college, having graduated from local high schools. Seven of the tutors went on to graduate from UC San Diego; four are now teachers.

Never have teachers serve more than two hour shifts in the HWC and never more than twice a week. What kind of teacher is going to be any good as a tutor if she's been teaching from 8 p.m. to 3 p.m. and then spends another four hours in the library?! If your HWC, like ours, is open 16 hours a week after school, between four and ten different math teachers are needed. Tutoring and supervising a busy HWC is hard work, so teachers deserve adequate compensation.

Demand consistent enforcement of rules and policies, including focused tutoring at all times. While the HWC must be a "positive" environment, it also must tolerate no "off-task behavior." This rule applies to college tutors who, during "slow" moments, may want to study for their own classes and to teachers who may be tempted to grade papers. Do not tolerate students' use of electronic devices or eating, drinking, or gum chewing.

Strictly adhere to accountability measures. Students must sign in and out of the HWC, indicating their name, the subject for which they came to get help, the arrival time, and the departure time. On the same sheet, teachers and tutors should write their names and arrival and departure times. These sheets can be used to track payroll information, and they can be kept in a centrally located notebook for teacher or parent reference.

Students only receive HWC slips when they demonstrate to teachers or tutors what they did with their time in the HWC; the slip has the date, student's name, time in and out, subjects addressed, a comments section, and teacher or tutor signature. The comments section allows the teacher or tutor to provide brief notes regarding what the student did in the HWC. Some teachers allow students to submit work one day late if it is accompanied by a HWC slip; some give extra credit to students for attendance. Parents, via the HWC slip, have proof of a student's participation in tutoring.

Give one person responsibility for maintaining HWC operations. A reliable person, someone with ongoing contact with teachers and tutors, should be responsible for maintaining the HWC's operation, including posting and collecting sign-in sheets, preparing payroll requests, readying the library for tutorial services, and ensuring availability of supplies.

Common Assessments in Mathematics

A primary goal of the SMART grant was to improve teachers' ability to collect, analyze, and use various data to improve classroom practice. Demystifying math education could only happen through study of empirical data that might force people to reconsider what they had previously taken for granted. A key focus of initial SMART efforts was development and implementation of site-specific, teacher-designed common assessments in Algebra, Geometry, and Intermediate Algebra. These assessments were not ends in themselves. Instead, they were catalysts to rethinking our practices.

Site-generated common multiple-choice tests targeted to key standards for every grading period were an essential means of promoting teacher accountability and collaboration. A "lead" teacher for each math course worked with colleagues to develop 20 to 25 items. All teachers of a given course gave the test and forwarded their students' results to the lead teacher, who entered the scores into a spreadsheet that allowed for detailed item analysis. Teachers could see on what items their students had done best and worst; the teachers could also study variation among all students' results. Teachers trusted one another with this information; the last person to see those data was the site principal, who supported and understood the process. Teachers then analyzed these data during regularly scheduled department professional development days.

This experience alerted teachers to the challenges of meaningful assessment and forced them to more explicitly link students' grades to mastery of key knowledge and skills. This approach represented a contrast to the common practice of basing grades on class participation, homework completion, or attendance. Conversations shifted from "My grades are based on 50% tests, 25% quizzes, and 25% homework" to "Anybody who passes this class must be able to explain how the graph of this linear equation relates to a table of values." Holding all members of a teaching community, such as a school's math department, accountable for giving and publishing results of common assessments communicated the message that everybody was responsible for students' success in math.

Giving teachers authority to develop and implement common assessments showed that they could collaborate as professionals who could act collectively to produce change on behalf of their students. Instead of administering off-the-shelf tests, the process of developing and revising common assessments proved more valuable because it forced teachers to work together and justify decisions regarding what should be tested, how, and why. Teachers saw the benefits of working with their colleagues to create the tests, but perhaps more importantly, to trust one another enough to submit their students' results for collective analysis. Collegiality was a prerequisite for risk-taking, as teachers challenged the way math had been taught.

Integrating common assessment data within ongoing teacher professional development created an explicit link between student achievement and pedagogy. Through SMART funding, all math teachers met twice each semester for professional development off campus, where they addressed common assessment data and instructional strategies.

Administrators promoted trust by recognizing the complex nature of both teaching and testing. Further, they never used the results from common assessments in evaluative contexts.

Math teachers from Calexico High School, another CAPP school, were willing to buy copies of the CVH math curriculum and assessments. The teachers were impressed by the curriculum mapping documents used to prepare for administration of common assessments. The curriculum maps included "sample assessment items" representing the kinds of questions students could expect to encounter each grading period.

However, I convinced Calexico's lead math resource teacher, Lydia, that the way to proceed was not to "buy" a curriculum, but to consider engaging in a "coaching" arrangement with CVH teachers, who could help Calexico teachers develop similar programs. Calexico cancelled its order for new textbooks so it could adopt the same books CVH used, and the department began to replicate the SMART system of curriculum maps and common assessments. Lydia also planned and led professional development days, and Calexico teachers joined SMART teachers to critique the rigor of their assessments during a week-long summer workshop. A WASC accreditation team member visiting Calexico High one year after the school's collaboration with CVH said that the math department's progress since the previous visit played a major role in the school's accreditation term. At Calexico, where uncertainty and change prevailed, including no permanent principal, a radical change in the bell and master schedules, and new textbooks, SMART's focus on assessments seemed to be a life buoy for dedicated, experienced, but potentially cynical math teachers.

Attempting to implement a system of common assessments would have been impossible for Calexico teachers had they not been matched with colleagues at CVH. What follows are some of the most important and practical lessons SMART schools have learned from their common assessment adventure.

Leadership of common assessment activities must come from teachers, not administrators. Each course should have a "lead" teacher with at least one period of time reassigned to leadership of curriculum development, alignment, and assessment activities. This person must have content knowledge and people skills and must understand the project's "big picture" as well as her or his role. Lead teachers must participate in district meetings, so they can connect site work to district-level initiatives. Failure to do this can result in a fatal disconnect from central authority that can doom the project. MVH relied on one full-time resource teacher to coordinate common assessment work for Algebra and Geometry. CVH provided four teachers with a "release period" so they could collaborate in Algebra, Geometry, and Intermediate Algebra work.

Administrators who controlled financial and human resources acknowledged the project's time-intensive nature, and they freed teachers from classroom responsibilities. Lead teachers did not teach full-time. SMART schools did not simply throw money at full-time teachers, expecting them to function in a leadership capacity without time to think, talk, or work. At CVH, each lead teacher had a job description, outlining specific expectations. These job descriptions were posted on the school's intranet, so every CVH teacher could see why these people had release time. Specific goals and indicators of progress made accountability much easier and protected the lead teachers from colleagues' envy.

While teacher leadership is essential in this process, so is support from competent administrators. The grant's goals were central to the School Site Plan. Every six weeks, I submitted a brief report regarding math department activities, and at the end of every semester, each lead teacher presented a portfolio of her or his work to the administrative team, so people could discuss what was or was not working. The discussions helped ensure that all school decision-makers understood the project and its achievements.

I eventually had to leave CVH when a new principal neither understood nor supported the work, and I transferred to Mar Vista High School which had a supportive principal. My CVH colleagues and I continue to implement common assessments through our partnership with Calexico High School and CAPP funding.

Teachers must begin common assessment work with clear goals, recognizing that the tests require revision at least annually. Recognizing that the assessments were intended to help teachers connect students' letter grades to demonstrated student proficiency, teachers at CVH decided to administer one common assessment of 25 multiple-choice items during each six-week grading period. Though teachers subsequently described limitations of the multiple-choice format, they accepted it because it allowed for item analysis.

At MVH, algebra and geometry teachers gave common assessments at least every three weeks. MVH teachers decided to include fewer questions and score student responses against a rubric. Individual teachers took turns developing each short test, and teachers often met to grade student work together.

Teachers at both sites appreciated frequent, relevant assessments that provided them with a better idea of what students know and can do. SMART sites accomplished this goal differently, but the project gave all teachers a chance to probe important issues. Teachers gathered to read and discuss student work; they shared materials and strategies, knowing what they hoped to accomplish during the semester. In addition SMART math teachers agreed to include one constructed-response item in their common assessments when they realized that the cognitive level addressed by most multiple-choice questions was far too low.

Teachers use the common assessments to help them engage in meaningful discussion about how and why they teach math the way they do. Using multiple-choice items on common assessments allowed teachers to perform item analysis of student results. Each teacher or lead teacher would score the answer sheets. The lead teacher for each course would compile an "item summary," assembling the data for every teacher, by period, by item on each assessment in a spreadsheet that allowed for a comparison of results by teacher, period, or item.

Discussion regarding the results might focus on the following questions: Why did so many students miss Question #4? Was the content of the question adequately addressed? Was the question's wording confusing? What about distractors offered as possible answers? Was Question #5 too easy? Did it really address content to be emphasized during a given grading period? Why did Teacher B's third period class do worse than her or his other sections? Why did Teacher A's students perform better than Teacher B's students? Allowing the data to prompt such questions enables teachers to discuss issues related to student achievement that they would not be able to do without defensiveness or fear of threatening their colleagues.

Most important, having data provides teachers a quantitative indicator of where their students are strong and where they are weak, so that teachers may modify future instruction accordingly. SMART schools have used these data in various ways, including developing "grade recovery" programs that allow students to present their teachers with alternative evidence of mastery of standards where they were previously weak. Teachers also compared these data with the CAHSEE, California Standards Tests, and Mathematics Diagnostic Testing Project tests to allow them to determine students' overall strengths and needs. Rather than simply becoming disempowered by the norm-referenced data that the state and district showered on them annually, SMART math teachers developed an internal, ongoing accountability system that provided them with meaningful information about where they and their students ought to go next. The assessments were site-generated and controlled, and teachers felt the assessments had meaning.

Grade Recovery Programs for Math

In most high school math programs, students who fail a math course are delayed in their required course sequence, and they also are more likely to encounter future academic difficulty. Schools often choose one of two options when faced with the specter of many failing students. First, the schools may require students to retake the semester they failed before allowing them to move ahead. This policy prevents students who have not yet mastered critical content from going forward. The other option is to allow students to advance to the second semester even if they earned grades of "D" or "F" in the first semester. At first, MVH and CVH teachers adamantly demanded that the "repeat" course of action be protected. They described how students needed to "learn a lesson" when they failed a math class, and they felt that forcing students to repeat a failed class taught students to work harder.

CVH departed from the "repeat" policy in 2002, opting to move all students from one semester to the next with the same teacher. One benefit of this policy change was reduced chaos in the school's second semester master schedule. Requiring students to take "repeat" courses not only complicated math scheduling, it wreaked havoc on the whole school's schedule and prevented many students from maintaining year-long courses. However, when the "repeat" policy ended, teachers complained that their second semester math courses contained students who "shouldn't be there," and they worried that students who had done well during the previous semester were being held back by less able classmates.

In the second semester of this policy change, CVH implemented its first "grade recovery" program. Second semester Algebra, Geometry and Intermediate Algebra classes are especially important for college admission. Students who earn a grade of "C" or higher in the second semester of one of these "A-G" courses can claim completion of an entire year of the course, regardless of their first semester grade. Students, therefore, had much to gain by "rescuing" their second semester grades. A "D" suffices for graduation, but not for college application purposes.

Believing that a students' letter grade in a math course ought to reflect what the student knows or can do, Algebra, Geometry and Intermediate Algebra teachers at CVH provided "grade recovery" workshops early in the semester. Recruited by teachers (including invitations sent home and delivered to class), students who had earned grades of "D" or "F" for the first progress reporting period participated in eight after-school hours of intensive work on standards that assessments revealed were students' greatest areas of need. If they attended all eight hours, students could take a constructed-response "grade recovery exam" covering the key concepts. Scored with a rubric developed by lead teachers and others in the department and returned to students' teachers, this exam provided students with another opportunity to demonstrate that they had, indeed, mastered key standards.

Teachers agreed to change the grades of students who participated—and succeeded—in the grade recovery program, reflecting both teachers' support of the program and their willingness to give students several opportunities to demonstrate their knowledge and skills. In addition to their students' attendance at the workshops, teachers received their students' exams, along with comments and rubric scores, so they could make the final decision about whether or not their students had, in fact, demonstrated knowledge and skills at an acceptable level. Teachers agreed that if a student earned a score of at least 80% on the recovery exam, then her or his six-week grade would change to a "C." A score of 90% resulted in a "B." Over 100 students voluntarily participated in each of the Algebra, Geometry, and Intermediate Algebra grade recovery programs that first semester, and about 75% of those students earned grades of at least "C" in the second semester course.

The goal of CVH's "grade recovery" program was to get students "back up on the horse" before the race was over. We did not want students with low six-week grades to give up when they might, after all, succeed. This intervention was different from programs that identified "at risk" students and placed them in special, remedial classes. Instead, students and teachers worked after school on a voluntary, but highly encouraged, basis to address standards where students had demonstrated weakness.

Central to this program's philosophy was the idea that students who received a "D" or "F" at the end of the first grading period had earned that grade because they lacked mastery of important knowledge or skills. Why not give them another chance to gain that knowledge? That teachers even agreed to try this program suggests that they had come a long way in their approach to grades.

Listed below are the most important characteristics of the grade recovery program, whose purpose was to promote success instead of stem a tide of failure. There is a big difference. Resources at SMART schools were focused on making the grade recovery program work, not on culling the flock of students to remove failures and track them into some lesser math course. This program is designed to do the following:

- Engage all stakeholders (math teachers, administrators, parents, and students) in a discussion that contrasts "reactive" interventions with programs that enable students to get the help they need to succeed in important classes the *first* time.

- Promote participation in a grade recovery program as a privilege. CVH teachers developed personal invitations for students and organized an assembly for all freshmen that featured prominent alumni and videos of graduation celebrations.

- Enlist motivating teachers to lead the workshops and recruit diverse members of the math department to contribute to construction and revision of grade recovery exams and other materials. The staff should be paid for their work, either during the summer or after school; they should also be rewarded with verbal accolades and public recognition.

- Monitor the results of grade recovery programs and publish them. People need to know if new programs are working and how success is defined. When CVH eliminated all "non-algebra" math courses, opting to place all ninth graders in Algebra or Geometry, instead of Pre-algebra or other non-"A-G" courses, the number of F's increased. However, almost twice as many students completed Algebra II than in previous years. There were more F's, but also more passing grades. When more students failed Pre-algebra than Algebra, nobody seemed particularly alarmed. Were these "throw-away" kids? Having a grade recovery program suggested to students and teachers that everybody could, in fact, succeed and that no losses were acceptable. The onus was placed on the students to extend the required effort, and those who did came out ahead.

- Educate counselors, teachers, and administrators about the program's purpose. People need to understand that this is not a "seat-time" program where students "do time" in exchange for higher grades. Discussing the program allows others to confront beliefs about which students should be expected to learn and reinforces the idea that a letter grade should have direct relationship to what students know.

Summer Acceleration Classes

Traditional summer school classes are usually reserved for students who lack credits due to previous course failures. Students can "make up" a grade for a course they failed during the regular year. Both students and teachers share the perception that success in summer school is much more closely related to attendance, seat time, and behavior than it is to mastery of essential standards. Any SUHSD student can tell you that a student cannot miss more than three whole days (or 12 hours of class) during summer school to earn credit for the course. Students are much less specific about what learning they must demonstrate to earn a passing grade. Seldom, if ever, do students enjoy the opportunity to *accelerate* their learning during the summer, and chances of acceleration are even more remote the higher up the academic chain students get, particularly in math and science.

SMART's central tenet that students should be expected to succeed the first time they are faced with a challenge led project leaders to develop a plan to expand access to acceleration opportunities in conjunction with the regular summer school program. The first effort failed when, just before the summer of 1998, project leaders were told that, "there were union problems" with the proposal, so "the district" would not allow the courses to be offered.

In 2000, SMART leaders advanced a second proposal, but we did more homework in advance. We proposed one section of Algebra and another of Intermediate Algebra, both located at CVH, where regular summer school would also occur. We overcame the union concern by consulting with everybody well in advance, opening consideration for the shared teaching assignments to teachers from all SMART schools, limiting participation in the program to students from SMART schools, and providing financial support for materials and human resources that helped the regular summer school program. SMART funds also supported one section of Music Theory/Piano, which benefited students in the School for the Creative and Performing Arts. The result? Almost 90% of participating students passed the classes with grades of "C" or higher, and all but five advanced to the next level of math, where they also earned passing grades.

In 2001, we proposed additional offerings for the SMART Special Summer. Initially, we were only going to offer math, as before. However, we learned that most CVH students failed to qualify for CSU/UC admission, lacking one credit of *science*. With the CVH science department chair, we examined why only 120 out of almost 600 students took Biology, and we decided to offer a summer accelerated Biology class to give more students access to that subject. Thus, we offered Algebra, Intermediate Algebra, Biology, Chemistry, and Music Theory/Piano. This time, the student response was overwhelming. We had waiting lists for every course. Over 56 students earned passing grades in each science course that summer, which contributed about a 20% increase in the annual CVH science course completion rate.

We had many discussions about selection criteria for each course, and we ultimately offered second sections of the science classes that accommodated nearly all applicants. Almost all students succeeded, even those whose traditional indicators, i.e., grade point average or standardized test scores, might have suggested otherwise. Not only did students pass the summer science classes; they also scored higher than "regular-year" students on the SUHSD common end-of-course exam. Students engaged in science learning for four-and-a-half hours every day for almost seven weeks, exactly 156 hours, as demanded by the SUHSD science lead teacher.

During summer 2002, we again offered Algebra, Intermediate Algebra, Biology, and Chemistry, but we added Geometry and Math Analysis. Over 300 students participated in the program, which operated concurrently with the regular summer school.

Again, students succeeded in overwhelming numbers, despite the deliberate decision not to screen students out of Algebra. The major focus of the 2002 program was transition to high school, and project leaders targeted outgoing eighth-graders to participate in Algebra and Geometry. Middle school students and teachers discussed the creation and implementation of classes, particularly Geometry, and we learned how projects like SMART could raise expectations for student achievement. We offered differentiated outcomes for students in the course: an "honors" designation attached to the grade if students participated in twice-weekly, project-based workshops. Parents and prospective students thronged to orientation meetings; teachers who had been involved in previous Special Summer efforts eagerly shared assignments with each other.

One might think that all this was positive news for the general SUHSD educational community, but each year I was astounded by the possibility of the program being derailed for myriad reasons. I had learned how to troubleshoot potential adversaries. Data on previous pass rates and exam scores were always published. I bit my tongue when people predicted that students "were not ready" to engage in algebra for seven weeks. I let the data speak for the program: 70% of the Algebra students earned a "C" or higher, and all of those students went on to take Geometry, and all of those students earned grades of "C" or higher. As a result of these courses, 65 freshmen took Intermediate Algebra during the school year, one year ahead of grade-level placement, and all advanced to Math Analysis, having earned grades of "C" or higher.

The next year, administrative and logistical obstacles loomed large, and despite the uproar from students and parents, no Special Summer program was offered. The outgoing CVH principal arbitrarily denied project leaders access to his site for Special Summer classes. Initially, he was affronted when we proposed using MVH as an alternate site. Then, two weeks later, he decided that the program could not take place at any site. The end of the Special Summer program, in light of its success, was disappointing to many.

Special Summer classes benefited over 900 students. However, the program's value went far beyond passing grades. Some of the most important lessons we learned from the Special Summer experience are listed below.

Students will rise to a challenge: Students were overwhelmingly willing to give up their summer to advance their academic coursework. These courses offered the rigor of intensive study, along with same account-ability measures applied to the traditional courses. Students invested significant effort and did well.

Students want to succeed, and when schools create opportunities for success, they communicate an essential belief that their kids can win: Schools need places where students who want to "do the right thing" can do just that. That so many students succeeded in acceleration courses flies in the face of arguments that students are lazy or disinter-ested. The "buzz" behind the Special Summer program communicated a positive expectation for learning. Students wanted to attend summer school. It was an honor, a challenge, a meaningful and voluntary dis-play of motivation. It was "cool" to say you were taking Chemistry.

Schools must explore and study alternative learning environments: The status quo, especially in schools serving large numbers of marginalized students, fails in too many regards. Many people questioned the idea of offering Algebra 1-2 during one seven-week summer term. The same people suggested that a Biology 1-2 course would never be the same as a "regular year" course. On a survey students stated that the classes were "fast" paced, but that immersing themselves in one subject made "real learning" possible. The summer biology students actually com-pleted more hands-on labs than students in regular-year classes. When we added up the hours of regular-year science instruction and considered the realities of 50-minute periods, testing, assemblies, and other interruptions, we found that the Special Summer students actually enjoyed MORE instructional time.

Schools must question traditional beliefs about placement and transition of students, especially regarding "high academic capital" courses like Algebra and Biology: The same people who suggested that seven weeks was not enough time to teach Algebra were adamant that we should not accept all applicants to the program. The candidates for the Algebra class were, in fact, enrolled in an "Algebraic Concepts" course in eighth grade and were already a year behind grade level, according to the state. However, their eighth-grade math course was designed to ground students in the more critical *conceptual* bases of algebra, so these young people were actually ideally situated to take an intensive, formal Algebra course. The fact that we encountered such resistance from adults and received such stony silence in response to positive results only hints at the many ways access to higher-level math is restricted.

Teachers function more effectively when they have support, respect, and flexibility: Once we had established the minimum number of hours that students would have to participate in Special Summer classes, many other decisions were left to teachers. For example, the science teachers agreed to do at least two complete labs a week, which resulted in most students experiencing between 14 and 20 labs, at least as many as students completed during the regular year. Special Summer teachers used their periods of over four hours to integrate lab work within regular instruction. They also extended the day for two hours twice a week to provide students with six-hour blocks to conduct experiments. Visitors to the program were impressed by the students' engagement despite being in the same class all day.

We hired a lab assistant to set up and tear down the labs. She met with teachers daily to adjust the lab schedule to the pace of each class, and she purchased and inventoried all supplies and equipment. She often helped provide feedback on student work and participated in classes. Her assistance allowed teachers to attend to students' learning. The lab assistant cost less than $2000 for the summer, under $10 an hour. The value added to the program far exceeded that minimal cost.

Acceleration programs serving incoming ninth-grade students support meaningful articulation between middle schools and high schools: This is because they focus on positive expectations for student success, with

teachers at both levels playing important roles. Perhaps the most exciting aspect of the last Special Summer session was how middle school
and high school teachers worked together to design classes for incoming
ninth graders. SMART project leaders arranged class visits with middle
school math teachers to inform students about the program and recruit
participants.

One surprise was the CVH counselors' resistance to the Special
Summer program. The counselors discouraged interested students.
"It's going to be really fast," the counselors warned. "Probably not a
good idea." Needless to say, this produced some confusion. Their low
expectations for students galvanized the will of teachers to get Special
Summer classes packed.

When over 80 students applied for Geometry, all but five expressed
intent to pursue the "honors" designation. We found money to support three teachers working with two sections of students and hired a
recent UC San Diego math graduate to provide twice-weekly enrichment workshops for those interested in earning an "honors" credit.
She helped the teachers design projects that emphasized application of
formal geometry, and only two students failed to successfully complete
the course. In the project's second year, one high school teacher and
one middle school teacher team taught the Algebra class. The resulting
curriculum and instruction were born of incredible discussions regarding how best to teach that important subject.

*The norms of traditional high school programs, including summer
school, present considerable obstacles to innovation:* Ironically, students who want to spend their summers engaged in meaningful learning have few opportunities. Significant resources are poured into traditional summer school programs where a student's only qualification for
participation often is previous failure. In the SUHSD, a full-time administrator oversees summer school, and she is paid throughout the year, at
least $100,000.

Students are labeled by their failure, and these labels are hard to shed.
We capitalized on their existence, though, when procuring matching
funds. We learned that the state provides "Beyond the Bell" funding to
"remediate" students who are "below grade level." We researched the
test scores of participating students and identified students who "qualified" for this money. Of course, we never told students which ones were
funded by what source, but we were able to fund two additional science
sections and the second Geometry section. Again, the vast majority
of students succeeded in Special Summer classes, and we found little

relationship between students' success and their previous standardized test scores.

The support of district staff is imperative so that arbitrary decisions do not terminate promising innovations: A nameless, faceless district authority rejected the first Special Summer effort. The second time around, we consulted with anybody who had the power to kill the program, including those who could influence would-be assassins. We acknowledged our vulnerability in trying to provide a new and challenging opportunity for students and teachers. We talked with the union representatives at all SMART sites as well as the head of the SUHSD teachers' union. We negotiated with SUHSD Food Services personnel regarding cafeteria support. We brought chocolate to the SUHSD payroll clerks, the people who made sure summer school staff received checks. We sent prospective course syllabi to the SUHSD Director of Curriculum and lead math/science teachers; we arranged for our Special Summer students to take the same end-of-course exams as "regular" students and reported results to SUHSD's Research and Evaluation staff. We got the support of our Area Superintendent, CVH principal, and the SUHSD Summer School Director.

Program evaluation, including publishing results, garners support, or at least toleration, from diverse members of the educational community: Special Summer's successes might have gone unrecognized had it not been for an almost obsessive level of documentation. We used an Excel spreadsheet to track data regarding program participation, and we analyzed these data to determine if we were achieving project goals. For example, we pulled test data for participating students, including grade point averages, CAHSEE results, and end-of-course-exam scores, and added Special Summer data as well as information on how students did after exiting the program. Of all the data elements, these later data were perhaps the most important. Not only did most of our students successfully complete Special Summer classes, they also went on to enroll in subsequent courses and earned passing grades in them as well. Again, presenting all stakeholders with data regarding students' performance was perhaps the most effective strategy for preserving the longevity of summer acceleration classes.

Negotiation among teachers, parents, administrators, counselors, and students supports a fluid innovation that responds to changing needs and concerns: The fact that a team of people organized and managed this program meant that many individuals had input into decisions. For example, we capitalized on regular summer school programs when they were offered at SMART schools. We asked these programs' administrators what kinds of support they would appreciate and worked out ways to get our project's needs met. We provided clerical help in exchange for the registrar entering our students' grades into the mainframe computer. We paid for an instructional aide (math major at UCSD, bilingual in Spanish and English) to provide two hours of after-school math tutoring. In exchange, we received use of facilities and custodial services. We bought some light bulbs for overhead projectors, and in exchange we were allowed to use the science lab rooms, equipment, and supplies, which we replaced at the end of the summer through SMART funds. Parents helped determine the days and hours for extended science classes, and the counselors helped route students to Special Summer classes during the registration period. We offered more classes each year and conducted more detailed monitoring of the program. We were able to obtain matching funds from several sources.

We worked as a team; each site leader or prospective Special Summer teacher had her or his ears open to possible challenges and new information. We pooled our intelligence. We made collective decisions that included defining admission criteria, opening additional sections, scheduling instructional time, and providing support services like the lab assistant and after-school tutoring. Together we managed to detect and address potential challenges before they destroyed the project. We knew we all had a lot to gain from the classes. Most importantly, we were motivated by what our students—and schools—would gain.

The use of various funding sources demonstrates a shared commitment to the goal that all students can succeed through the collective actions of many: Using various funds requires that the program managers first learn that the money exists. Therefore, I worked with people at each SMART school who had the "bird's eye" view of all the supplemental and grant funding. Most often, this person was the Categorical Coordinator who developed and reviewed the annual School Site Plan. Integrating SMART goals within each school's Site Plan was very important in our effort to institutionalize the Special Summer program.

The initiatives discussed here—the tutoring and homework center, common assessments in mathematics, the grade recovery program for math, and summer acceleration classes—are all grounded in the imperative: expect success. Students and teachers may struggle, falter, and tire in this teaching and learning dance. But we have got to set the bar higher for ourselves and our students and know that by building on success, we are diminishing failure. We must learn, not just to do more, but to do better. And we cannot lose heart, because if we do, we will be losing students' futures.

❖   ❖   ❖

Commentary

ZELDA GLAZER

Zelda Glazer *(former Director of Curriculum, Dade County School District) began this commentary shortly before her untimely death in an automobile accident.* Alice Kawazoe *completed the commentary from Glazer's notes and taped remarks.*

Expect success? Most large urban school districts expect failure, so that any progress can be judged as exceeding expectations. Perhaps this mentality is the result of perpetual educational backpedaling, of educational institutions constantly defending themselves against onslaughts from the outside. Reaction rather than innovation becomes the hallmark of our school systems.

After Sputnik in the late 1950s, we plunged headlong into fortifying our math and science instruction to produce more and better scientists; in the post-Vietnam era, we discovered our students couldn't read, so we fell back onto phonics and scripted reading programs. In the midst of the No Child Left Behind era, we are caught in the web of accountability, judged by district, state, and federal assessments that measure the progress and regress of students at every grade level. In reaction, test preparation and "remediation" classes dominate the curriculum. Currently, the movement is toward disassembling comprehensive high schools into "small learning communities," under the assumption that "small is beautiful," or at least more beautiful than big.

So, after more than 45 years of being buffeted and bashed by the latest mandate, reform, imperative, movement, program improvement, and threat, how refreshing for this jaded soul to read this vigorous case study by Katrine Czajkowski. Her call to expect success, rather than accede to failure, is more than a naïve paean to the power of positive thinking. And she is not a glass half-full, rose-colored-glasses-wearing optimist. She's not asking us to "look on the bright side" of things or to "make lemonade out of lemons." As we sit in our crowded classrooms, difficult schools, and plodding bureaucracies, she calls to us to turn our thinking upside down, to stand on our heads.

She challenges us not to get new glasses, but to get new eyes. She asks us not to look at our students as lemons, reduced to pulp by squeezing, but to see them as full glasses, brimming over with need. And most difficult of all, she demands that we examine the "dark side" of what we do and the debilitating effects of our shallow thinking, poor planning, and expedient practice.

As a friend of mine would say, "She's an activist—one of those pushy broads," and for him, that's a compliment. This "pushy broad" writes a letter to the university that gave her a teaching credential, chiding them for not preparing her to teach her students. I felt that same inadequacy after my first year of teaching, too, but instead of acting on my frustration, I just sobbed frequently.

Throughout this case study is a tone of persistence and assertiveness, like the tune in your head that won't go away. But this is the persistence of a very smart woman, who has bright ideas and learns the pragmatism of her profession, who learns how to get things done—in short, an activist. I suspect that her assertive activism threatened the principals who did not support common assessments and who terminated the Special Summer program. One smart woman and another persistent woman they could tolerate, but a young, articulate, visionary woman of action would be too much for them to handle, too great a threat to their leadership.

A few words here about leadership in high schools. We often bemoan the fact that high school administrators expend their energies and time on crisis management, safety, and operations, so that they have little left for instructional leadership. My major concern is not about instructional leadership. If administrators are blessed with a Katrine, or a cluster of lesser versions of her, then they just need to give those teachers opportunities to improve and strengthen the curriculum and instructional program and support the teachers' efforts with funding, release time, planning time, paid assistance, and encouragement.

My greater concern is the paucity of *intellectual leadership*. Because of pressures and dangers, both real and perceived, principals tend to be conservative types, bereft of audacity, content to maintain the status quo rather than venture into new territory. Or their versions of innovation are spin-offs of old ideas: borrowing sustained silent reading from elementary grades; implementing an advisory period that resembles the old homeroom; and reverting to a practice popular decades ago—

stretching the Algebra I curriculum over two years, so slower students
can learn more slowly.

My purpose here is not to criticize sustained silent reading, adviso-
ries, or two-year algebra, but we must recognize that they are insufficient remedies to the maladies that afflict struggling high school
learners. Most principals at some point face the wall of insufficiency
and lament, "We've done all these things, instituted all these programs,
and still all our students aren't achieving at high levels." An intellectual
leader understands the notion of insufficiency—good, but not good
enough—and pushes and probes to reach what Shakespeare calls "the
undiscovered country." A bold, thoughtful leader finds a way to break
through or scale the wall of insufficiency and leads the staff to discover
what best serves the needs of students and advances their learning, and
more importantly, compels the staff to examine its own values and
attitudes about students, teaching, and learning.

Most of the programs Katrine discusses are ubiquitous in high
schools. But the philosophical and pedagogical underpinnings of each
program she describes are antithetical to most of what we do in high
school. She pushes us to think about how to recreate and re-envision
schooling—program by program, practice by practice—such as the
homework center and summer school.

High schools have had study halls and after-school tutoring for eons.
Most often students are "sent" to the homework center as punishment
for excessive tardies, absences, or misbehavior, or they are forced to
attend to make up assignments and take tests. Or it is place where
athletes are sent to raise their grades to maintain eligibility. A damn-
ing jailhouse vocabulary emerges about homework centers: Students
need to "serve time" or "serve detention" or "seat time." The center
becomes a "holding pen," a place "for trouble-makers to sit out their
time." One homework center I visited had posted signs demanding,
"No talking. No eating or drinking. No walking around. Do not dis-
turb other students or staff."

But the Tutoring and Homework Center described here is a positive
place to learn, where students can get one-on-one tutoring or small
group help from a teacher, college student, or knowledgeable high
school student. Students are not forced to attend, but they come voluntarily, taking responsibility for their learning. They work for at least
30 minutes, leave when they need to, and receive slips noting date, time
of attendance, and help received to get "credit" for their participation.
The premise of this Tutoring and Homework Center is that students

want to be successful; they want to learn, and they will seek help to improve their learning. Voluntary learning instead of forced learning, learning time instead of jail time, are important aspects of the "Expect Success" Homework Center.

The summer school described here is not a time to step backward, but to step forward, not for remediation, but acceleration, not to make up credits, but to gain credits by taking legitimate courses, not in a truncated, diluted form, but full blown and demanding. Teachers often grumble about summer school classes as "lesser versions" of regular-year courses and ask, "How can students get full credit for just six weeks of instruction?" Katrine's answer is to redefine and revolutionize summer school: extend the instructional hours, increase the rigor of the classes, accelerate learning, and provide necessary student support so that teachers can plan and work collaboratively and be innovative, and most importantly, so that students can experience advanced learning and success.

Further, Katrine apparently collects data like a demon. She uses data to improve practices and programs, substantiate successes, evaluate effectiveness, and she publishes and shares the results with fearless transparency. She is an exemplar of "data-driven decision-making," generating, collecting, and analyzing data; making changes after analysis; and publishing results—leaving a numbers trail as evidence of the impact of her innovative initiatives.

What I like most about Katrine—her thinking, actions, and case study—is her audacity. Think. Act. Change. Push no students to the margins of education for the margins are empty space. She implores us to expect success from all students—and shows us how to do it. She's "an activist . . . a pushy broad" of the highest order.

❖ ❖ ❖

Commentary

ALAN WEISBERG

During the past several years of working with her, I've come to expect success from Katrine Czajkowski in most every new project she takes on. She is a rare teacher who somehow finds time to stay current on the never-ending national quest to reform public education. Her interests include policy and pedagogy, and she approaches both with an appropriately critical eye. Above all, she dedicates herself to being an outstanding teacher for those she calls "marginalized students of color." She refuses to give up on the large public high schools that these students attend despite their banal realities. "Expect Success" is her effort to describe in terms that are useful to both policy makers and teachers some of the results of the work she and her colleagues have done, sponsored by CAPP, at two big high schools in the Sweetwater Union High School District in southern California.

I take some pride in my role both in monitoring some of the CAPP grants that Katrine directed, and more importantly, for urging her to get some of the lessons learned on paper. I did this because so much of her work directly addresses many of the concerns I constantly hear from teachers at the low-performing schools I work with: How can you get kids to work harder and be motivated to learn the basics? What does it take to get more kids to succeed in higher level math? How can teachers support each other's efforts to succeed more often with more students?

In my own school reform work, I often find that even after some intensive work with a single school over a few years, little has changed. Old patterns re-emerge when incentive funding for reform dwindles away or one or two dynamic leaders leave. The most intractable characteristic of the kind of high schools that Katrine and I work with is low scores on standardized achievement tests.

Because of the ever-increasing pressure from state and federal levels to improve scores or suffer the punishment of sanctions and take-over, schools leap to short-term, short-thought remedies that cannot be sustained. These remedies rely on temporary funding or are born from desperation rather than cogent planning and long-term thinking. Instead of asking the question, "How do we raise CAHSEE and CST (California Standards Test) test scores?" Katrine tries to answer the larger, more challenging question, "How do we support the learning of marginalized, struggling students?" She is banking on the contention that by answering the second question, schools will, over time, answer the first. However, simply implementing the principles and practices discussed in her case study is not the silver bullet that will produce quick, significant increases in standardized test scores.

But I don't think we need test score evidence to justify the value of having an inviting place for students to do their homework and get help and tutoring after school. Or offering willing students the opportunity to accelerate their studies of math or science during the summer. Or getting math teachers to agree upon what should be regularly tested during the course of a year of algebra or geometry.

Katrine does as good a job as any teacher or administrator I've known in taking seriously the commitment to what has come to be known in the jargon of the school reform world as "using data to drive improvement." Her tables and charts measuring progress are legion among the folks who work with her. She likes to measure progress and is compelled to find some objective way of judging success or failure. She believes in accountability by those who administer discretionary funds (including budget transparency), and by the teachers who get to try new things with such money. Project directors must have a detailed job description. Reform efforts need clearly articulated goals, and not too many of them. Planning and work meetings must have a note-taker, and minutes that highlight who commits to doing what need to go out quickly. These and other seemingly obvious principles for reform are well covered in her case study along with the "how to" sections that tell how to start and run a homework center or run grade recovery classes.

Katrine has her biases and is not afraid to put them front and center. Let me mention just three: tracking is a disaster; the status quo exists to be challenged; and teacher collaboration is a must. I mention these because while I agree with each, I would venture to guess that when pushed, many, if not a majority, of the teachers in the schools where we work do not.

These three principles are commonly shared by those who write about reforming urban high schools. Tracking, of course, holds back many potentially successful students, and passing judgments on ninth graders about who is "college material" and who is not tends to be self-fulfilling. Most teachers in these schools would agree on the broad principle. But when I describe to math teachers the practice at one CAPP-supported school of having all ninth graders study algebra in heterogeneous groups, I am met by blank stares or downright pity for the poor teachers who must do this. Or if I suggest to talented social studies teachers that their AP history and government classes drain classrooms of many students whose presence in mainstream classes would enhance teaching and learning for all, similar reactions emerge. One of the rewards for longevity as a teacher in high schools is the opportunity to teach the successful students who are clustered together in advanced classes. Who can blame a teacher with 150-plus students and five classes a day for looking forward to teaching these classes? The natural pattern, the default, at most high schools is to track students based on past performance.

Katrine's belief that the status quo needs to be challenged doesn't have much currency among the teachers I've worked with over the years, except when it comes to banding together to guard against arbitrary and unfair actions by administrators that affect teachers' working conditions—and then the challenge is through collective bargaining agreements rather than through the actions of individuals. Katrine's belief in the importance of teacher collaboration may be shared by many teachers, again as a general principle. But collaboration takes time, the one commodity in short supply at the high schools I have seen. If teachers strongly held the belief that teaching and learning in high schools would improve through collaboration with their colleagues, they would fight for more time to work together—and challenge the status quo. In general, I don't find high school teachers to be big risk takers in the realm of improving conditions for their students. The impetus for more time for collaboration usually comes from the urging of reform entities like the Coalition of Essential Schools, other foundation/grant-supported groups, or WASC reviews, not from the demands of teachers.

Values, not cookbook instructions, are at the core not only of the principles mentioned in the early part of the case study, but also in the detailed discussions of implementing the reforms. I came to realize this most vividly at a school outside of California—call it Interstate High—where I've taken the lead in starting a homework center based on Katrine's experience and perspective. I've seen too many tutoring centers that are extra-pay subsidies for contracted teachers rather than places for students to improve their learning. The centers are punitive and often reflect the worst of classroom management techniques.

To create a positive, successful homework center at Interstate, I circulated the section of "Expect Success" that deals with the homework center to key teachers and administrators. Interstate is a relatively small (700 students) school with among the lowest test scores in its state. I easily convinced some willing teachers that Katrine's advice should not be taken lightly. But I failed to get the message across to the principal.

In its first pilot phase, the homework center at Interstate failed to find college tutors or enough teachers and other volunteers to meet the math needs of students who showed up. The *value* of having college students not just as tutors but also as role models simply didn't sink in, even with the best of the teachers.

Another issue faced by the school's new homework center was whether or not football players could be forced to attend. The school principal knew full well that football success was much valued by her supervisors, and she wanted to force all football players to attend each day before practice so their GPAs didn't fall below the district-mandated level to play. The problem was forcing them to attend, mixing them with students who showed up voluntarily. For the homework center to work, it shouldn't be mandatory. Positive reinforcement like sending information on attendance and accomplishments at the center to teachers provides incentives for learning. Negative reinforcement—in this case attend the homework center or you can't play ball—becomes punitive. People learn with greater ease when they want to learn. Convincing the principal of this reality will be a challenge. Football players are welcome and should be urged to attend, but only if they decide to do it themselves.

In an early visit to the center, I witnessed a disconcerting violation of several of Katrine's guiding principles. One of the biggest problems at the school is a group of experienced teachers who have been at the school for a long time and have never abandoned their aggressive, blaming attitude towards students. In choosing teachers to work at the center, we carefully avoided these people, but even with pay for teachers, there weren't enough teachers due to the tutor shortage and the success in drawing students. So, one of the old-guard teachers was hired. In front of my face she began yelling and demeaning one of the students at the center and made the student leave for what appeared to me to be little more than loudness. A reprimand may have been appropriate, but a loud, public one was not, and if that sort of environment becomes dominant at the center, attendance will surely drop off until the entire effort will not be worth all the work involved.

From my experience with the people responsible for running summer schools, I fear Katrine's idea of using summer school not just as a remedial exercise (which the state is willing to pay for) but as an opportunity to help willing students accelerate their studies (which state funding formulas do not support) will not be easily embraced. Most educators I work with, including the vast majority who care about kids and about doing a good job, have an aversion to challenging the status quo even in the form of state funding formulas.

The state may not think that acceleration is worth funding, but that doesn't mean that accelerated summer classes are forbidden. The kinds of schools Katrine addresses in her chapter almost always have discretionary resources that, if used with some creativity, can make needed changes happen. While in California the state is the major funder for schools, it is not the only one. And despite federal and state mandated testing and sanctions, the law supports local control. While the lack of state support will be the stated reason, I suspect that resistance to change and innovation, and in the worst instances, lethargy may make it unlikely that many schools will seek to establish accelerated summer classes. I would love to be proven wrong.

So much of what Katrine writes is about overcoming a deficit model—that is, students are behind and need to be remediated. Thus, for example, summer school becomes a large enterprise for all the failing students, who reluctantly attend often with similarly reluctant teachers motivated primarily by summer pay. We clearly need more teachers and administrators capable of advancing a vision of a different kind of summer school that helps students on the margin tip over into success. I hope that Katrine's words can motivate at least a few.

For me, the most delightful aspect of Katrine's thinking is her cry to end the deficit model of instruction. Now, with No Child Left Behind sanctions, hundreds of schools, or in some cases whole districts, are in "program improvement," which is interpreted as: get those scores up and do it fast. The practical reforms she describes are part of a change in thinking about students and a longer-term strategy to improve teaching and learning.

At another school that CAPP serves, the faculty's philosophical statement about students goes well beyond the ubiquitous mission statement that "All students can learn" and replaces it with: "All students are smart." Bringing out the intelligence in all students is the job of good teaching. Simply buying new curriculum that will help students get better test scores is not reform.

We now live with an impatient system that is not satisfied with gradual improvement, the sort that can result from longer-term strategies—and deeper and more lasting strategies—like the ones suggested by Katrine. Schools are caught in a dilemma: the need to make long-term, significant changes to advance student learning and the need to meet short-term, mandated gains in standardized testing scores.

"Expect Success" responds to this dilemma by putting energy into the first need and counting on the residual effect those efforts will have ultimately on the second.

Coaching in Mathematics

Teachers, Departments, and Schools

BARBARA WELLS

COACHING IS A TYPE of on-site intensive support that CAPP can provide. Barbara Wells, a recently retired math professor from the University of California, Los Angeles, has the expertise, acumen, and people skills to work effectively with individual teachers, departments, and administrators to improve math instruction. In so doing, she also gets the staff to pay attention to raising academic and behavioral standards; she delights in small successes. She negotiates agreements and continually presses teachers to rise above contentiousness and get down to the practical business of instructional improvement. She is a coach in the best sense of the word.*

❖ ❖ ❖

This two-day visitation is a continuation of work begun the previous year. It is the ninth visit in a series that constitutes part of an intensive professional development program that CAPP sponsors for the mathematics faculty at Coastline High School.

PREPARATION

To prepare for this visit, I sent algebra curriculum binders to each member of the department as well as one for the algebra teacher at

*The names of the school and staff members have been changed in Wells's detailed log of two days of coaching.

the junior high school and a department reference copy. These binders contained department-created syllabi, pacing guides for each trimester of Algebra I, two benchmark tests at each level, all quizzes and tests for the course, grade sheets, assignment sheets, keys for quizzes and tests, and a log to record student out-of-class meetings for assistance. In our summer work, all teachers had agreed to increase the responsibility level for students. This effort included (1) focusing on every classroom minute as an instructional opportunity; (2) giving the long-range assignment sheet to raise student responsibility and decrease unfocused classroom activity; (3) providing students with the experience of learning something on their own without prior teacher introduction; and (4) attempting to standardize the Algebra I experience of all Coastline High School students. I sent all materials with lengthy notes to teachers regarding expectations for their instruction.

OBSERVATION

I was able to observe all mathematics teachers on one day. Two of them—Mr. A and Ms. B—were new to me, as they had not taught at Coastline the previous year. All teachers had their own classrooms, but several did not have textbooks for their students to have at home. With the initiation of the competency-based mathematics placement, some of the tenth graders were placed again in Algebra I classes—and not in geometry—and they needed these texts, causing a shortage of algebra texts. It would be important for teachers to prepare photocopies of the material for which students were responsible in those classes where texts were not yet available.

Ms. C: I observed part of this teacher's first and sixth period classes. In first period the class had been depleted by a language test that was occurring at that time. The teacher chose to use the time to review multiplication facts in the form of a bingo game. While this may be an innovative way of engaging the students, I was concerned that not moving forward with the next lesson would cause the students and teacher to fall behind in covering the required curriculum.

The sixth period was a specially designed academic instruction in English (SDAIE) algebra class. These ninth graders were struggling to learn how to solve simple equations using addition and subtraction. Problems of the following type were demonstrated and then practiced: $-14 = x + 6$ or $x - 21 = -18$ or $y + 13 = -4$. Students had trouble grasping the entire procedure conceptually because they: (1) had not grasped the meaning of additive inverses; (2) had not mastered addition and subtraction of integers and did not know how these two operations were related; and (3) were not clear on the reason for "solving" an equation. Hence, most of their struggle was reduced to mimicking what was demonstrated. Ms. C gave enough practice with different problems that several students demonstrated that they could solve an equation by the end of the period. However, it seemed possible that without a "review" the next day, the same students would not be able to solve comparable problems successfully. So, the teacher would need to continuously provide activities to address the weaknesses above in addition to providing ongoing practice in solving equations. These students were also further hindered by not having textbooks.

Mr. A: I observed part of this teacher's first period class. He was a first-year teacher, having just recently graduated. His class was controlled and listening to him when I arrived. During our ongoing conferences and professional development this year, I would encourage him to decrease the amount of class time devoted to "teacher talk" and to increase the explanations and elaborate on the concepts being taught. Examples:

> "You always want to do the opposite." (*What is the opposite? Why is it the opposite? Why do the opposite?*)

> "Adding and subtracting are opposites." (*Why? Are there any others? How will I know if two operations are opposites?*)

> "Let's do one more . . ." (*Instead of the teacher doing the problem one more time, have the students talk through the example or solve the problem.*)

In several of the classes I observed, teachers made a point of telling students to take notes on the lecture, and student participation was minimal or nonexistent. It's important for the teachers to explain the purpose of the notes, how they will be or should be used, and check that they are used constructively. Mr. A told the students to write a summary of their notes, and he would stamp their summary. I was encouraged by this strategy as a means of students synthesizing what he had delivered. He needed to give the students time to think about and write the summaries before checking and stamping the papers.

Ms. D: I observed part of this teacher's second period class. Ms. D is certainly a success story! Her developmental growth as a teacher since her start last year is astounding. Of all the teachers introducing equations today, she was the only one who used the balance scale in an active manner that engaged the students in making sense of the balance metaphor for solving equations. Her class was orderly, on task, and participatory. I was also impressed by the student-made charts on the walls, showing the words used to indicate the various mathematical operations. One chart of mathematical terms was also in Spanish. I look forward to her further progress. Because she is on such a meteoric arc, I want to push her to think about making other connections to topics she is introducing. For example, with the balance scales, one could ask: why does the figure in front of courthouses have a blindfold and carry a balance scale?

Mr. E: I observed part of this teacher's second period class. Rather than present the lesson on division of integers, Mr. E gave his students the opportunity to learn division by exploration. I wanted to stand up and shout, "Bravo!" I would encourage him to continue working on creating opportunities for students to participate more fully and to make his board presentations more legible. When he used a light green pen and erased, it left a green haze on the board; then when he rewrote with that same pen, the result was almost always illegible. Students complained, but he made a joke of it.

I observed that several of the teachers were not following one or more of the components of our agreed-upon protocol. It was not clear to me that the new teachers had been given an orientation regarding the Algebra I program; however, the teachers who participated in the summer program were familiar with and agreed to the protocols. In this case, I noted that Mr. E was not adhering to the use of the long-range assignment sheet as agreed upon. Additionally, since Mr. E had no textbooks for his class to use at home and no photocopies available for the students, his class was doing work that day that should have been done a week earlier.

Mr. F: I observed part of this teacher's third period Algebra II class. Evidently Mr. F had been absent recently, and the class had several assignments to review. When I arrived students were not on task, but Mr. F began class and went over the work they should have accomplished in his absence. Only about 60 percent of the class appeared to be engaged in the activity of checking work. Several had no papers in front of them or had not unpacked their backpacks. Others continued to carry on conversations. I would encourage Mr. F to increase opportunities for students to participate more fully and to make sure he checks more systematically for questions and understanding.

Mr. F then presented some ways to graph lines. I was surprised that he was encouraging students at this level to make T-charts to graph lines. He stated that rather than changing an equation in standard form to slope-intercept form (because many students get tripped up in that procedure), he promoted the idea that they find the x- and y-intercepts instead. Most mathematics educators would say that, at the Algebra II level, students should develop facility in manipulating the symbols to obtain a linear equation in a multiplicity of formats and that reliance upon T-charts should be decreased.

Mr. G: I observed part of this teacher's third period class. When I arrived the teacher was presenting the notes for the lesson on graphing on the overhead projector. The class was orderly and attentive. Mr. G demonstrated using three points for graphing a line and also wrote definitions of intercepts. I wished there had been more attempts at bringing the students into the conversation, making it a class activity rather than a teacher-centered lesson. Mr. G passed out graph paper to the students to use when attempting to graph the line. But many students were confused and did not know how to begin. I asked Mr. G why so many students did not seem familiar with the content. He stated that we "may have set the bar too high." When queried about out-of-class help, Mr. G said that his students were not coming in for help.

Ms. B: I observed part of this teacher's fifth and sixth period classes. She is the other new teacher in the department. She was animated and tried to assuage students' anxieties related to mathematics by personalizing examples and problems. I would encourage her to avoid personal examples and focus on mathematics examples more directly related to the students' experiences to avoid distracting student queries. Much of the teaching assumed a level of mathematical conceptual understanding that could not be guaranteed. It is important for Ms. B to assess her students' level of understanding as she moves forward with the curriculum. For example, "If you add to both sides of an equation, the result is an equivalent equation." Do all the students know what an "equivalent equation" is? Why is it important that it be an "equivalent equation"?

Although I would like to see Ms. B doing less of the work and students participating more, she did stress the importance of checking work, and she presented a four-step procedure for solving word problems that had potential. I will encourage her to decrease student reliance upon acronyms (e.g., WYDOOSOTEDOTO or "What you do on one side of the equation, do on the other") and give more thought to defining variables (e.g., *b* does not stand for the brother, but *rather the brother's age in years*). She will need assistance in managing the class when she is not talking to them in order to help them develop scholastic direction and independence.

Mr. I, the principal, was not available as he was attending a meeting at the county office. I have for some time wanted to speak with him about the school's use of students as teacher aides. Today I saw students serving in this capacity in five classrooms. Only in Ms. H's class did I see the assigned student (a senior) using time constructively. My question is: how can a low-performing school defend any student being allowed to lounge—literally and figuratively—for one period each day? Even if these students were reading a book or studying for a class when they were not performing a task for the teacher, one could argue that the assignment supported a modicum of self-improvement. But such was not the case here. Instead, "TA" students ate, chatted with students, entertained friends outside the classroom door, relaxed in the teacher's chair, and presented the class with a picture contrary to the scholastic effort we were trying to engender.

GENERAL OBSERVATIONS ABOUT CLASSROOM VISITATIONS

The teaching I observed consisted mostly of material distributed and the teacher lecturing with students supposedly taking notes. Do we have any proof that "telling" is equivalent to "learning" or promotes "knowing"? Evidence indicates that just the opposite is true. For example, words like "origin" provide an opportunity for students to connect their understanding of the word to its mathematical meaning.

In several classes I still saw the extent to which food and drink provided a significant distraction to the learning environment: (1) the sounds of crackling bags and aroma of chips divert adjoining students' attention from the lesson; and (2) hands that were involved in imbibing and ingesting were not writing notes or solving problems. Teachers appeared to concede defeat in second period because of its proximity to brunch. But why is food on such blatant display in just about every other class period as well? The Curriculum Leadership Council and administrators may want to discuss this issue and develop a common policy regarding food during class time.

COLLABORATIVE MEETING

I had composed an agenda for our meeting that provided opportunities for us to: (1) review and reflect upon the guiding principles of our work; (2) relate those objectives to our current situation; (3) provide instances where growth is evident (*e.g.*, Ms. D's classroom performance last year versus this year's); (4) discuss student performance on the first algebra benchmark test; (5) edit and revise benchmark tests; (6) reaffirm commitment to following protocols established during the summer; (7) check on logistics for use of computer labs; and (8) choose a department chairperson. I had been told that one of the vice-principals would join us for lunch to advise us regarding the new paid position of department chair. I agreed that it was no problem for her to have the time during our working lunch to make this presentation. I had also hoped that after lunch I would be able to have individual conferences with people about what I had observed in their classes. However, I did not have time to conduct these sessions.

Indeed, I recognized the agenda was overly ambitious. But after bringing the two new teachers up to speed with respect to what we were trying to accomplish, the weight of so many students not passing the first benchmark test took over and drove the rest of the agenda. Three issues emerged:

First, students were not coming in for help. We provided each student a grade sheet to record his or her quiz and test grades. On the reverse side was a place to log in every time they went to the Homework Center or to their teacher for assistance after school. Most teachers said that this had made no dent in the number of students who had come for help. The thinking appears to be that if it does not get done during the school day, then it is not going to be done.

Second, the mathematics teachers felt that, except for the science department, they were fighting the battle alone with respect to raising the academic standards, as well as changing the school's culture. Specifically, numerous comments were made about the AVID teachers who told the math teachers that they did not like how the algebra program prevented sections of their preferred courses from being offered. Department members sensed opposition to holding AVID students back if they did not pass their math benchmarks. Someone suggested that teachers wanted the students to meet the A through G requirements whether the student's knowledge actually supported what was recorded on the transcript. Someone asked if any research related to Coastline students' attaining a degree from a four-year college or university was available.

Finally, teachers expressed concerns about whether specific problems on the benchmark tests were too difficult. Some classes skipped a section by mistake, and we removed questions from the test related to that section. It was agreed that the next trimester that section should be included. The discussion extended to the nature of a benchmark test and whether or not it was "fair" to expect students to be given a cumulative test as a benchmark, since the current teacher may not have taught all of the test's content.

We spent most of the morning addressing these concerns. We agreed that all parents who come for progress reports should be informed about opportunities for extra help for their students. Students who failed the tests should be told they *must* come in for help and be assigned a particular day. Unfortunately, the AVID model does not require students to spend time outside the school day to address academic deficiencies. Students receive necessary tutoring during the school day, and a bit of a conflict is created when students assume that in-school tutoring is sufficient, and after-school work is unnecessary. We recognized that since these students are behind, the amount of daily homework might overwhelm some of them at first. But we felt that setting a pace that represented what is required for the algebra course and supporting students is better than slowing down and not accomplishing what the content standards mandate.

At one of our next meetings, we will try to collaborate with the science department and let them know what we are doing. Perhaps they could support aspects of our program and maybe we could support their work with students. Even though the math department is pessimistic about the outcome, we should do the same with the AVID teachers. I have heard nothing except that these teachers are super protective of their students. A conversation with the teachers might enlighten both sides. If we can shed some light about why we are proceeding as we are, and they can give reasons for why they object to what we are doing, we would be on the first step to helping the AVID students and, more significantly, helping all the students at the school. The Curriculum Leadership Council should discuss this issue, so that everyone clearly understands the math department's goals and how they are intended to raise expectations and achievement.

With regard to the benchmark tests, we went through each one that was recently given. We removed problems that the teachers felt were too difficult, and we will be revising the ones that determine which students will repeat their module. Each department member is on a committee to work on these tests. This part of the meeting was the most contentious because, sadly, several teachers felt that if the student has not seen the exact type of problem, then it is not "fair" to ask the problem on the test. I promised to research which problems came from which part of the publisher's assessment book, so the teachers would know that the problems were an expectation for students of this level. However, the fact that the teachers still saw mathematics as a procedure automatically approached in a given way—leaving no room for application—had implications for me about how they were teaching the material and what kind of support I might provide.

I must continue to try to communicate the "why" of mathematics instruction to the teachers. Once we have the same understanding of why we are teaching mathematics, then we will not be concerned about whether the assessment item is identical to something the students have seen multiple times in class, which is what the students often face on standardized tests.

When Mr. J, the assistant principal, arrived, the department shared its concerns about the likelihood that there might be many failures this first cycle of the competency-based algebra program. He suggested that we invite the administrative staff to meet with us to outline our concerns. The principal and both assistant principals attended.

We presented the facts that: (1) students were not coming in for help after class; (2) many students might have to repeat their current algebra module even if they did not fail the class; and (3) a larger number than usual might fail their algebra module because (as recommended) 40 percent of their trimester grade was represented by benchmark test performance. We asked to what extent the school community would support us if this occurred in a dramatically negative fashion. We had already agreed to give the counselors a list of potential repeaters four weeks before the end of the trimester. After much supportive discussion, all administrators gave their blessing to what we were trying to do. The principal said that he would try to arrange for the progress reports to have a check-off indicating the student had failed a benchmark test. He believed that could be done, but he would have to look into it for us. He also asked that two department members present the program as well as the rationale for it to the school board at its next meeting. He encouraged us to continue the collaboration with the algebra teacher at the middle school and said that it might even be worthwhile for him to join us at our CAPP meetings. The teachers received a thorough backing, and it appeared that the administration would do whatever possible to prevent this issue from becoming the political debacle it could potentially be. This program would require conscientious communication with parents as well as direct action with students. It would also mean providing daily quiz items and class work that stretch students' understanding beyond the mnemonic or one-step operation.

Mr. J relayed some good news to us before the meeting: the textbooks had arrived. A sigh of relief could be heard because in addition to the instructional necessity of each student having a textbook, the issue of insufficient numbers of texts could have added to the dissension related to a large number of students not passing benchmark tests.

Addendum

When I returned home I received a message from Ms. D regarding one of the procedures we instituted in Algebra I that related to grading: namely, the lowest test grade and the lowest quiz grade were both dropped when calculating the student's average. We did this so that students would be encouraged to be present for all tests and quizzes and also allow for students having a "bad day" for one test and one quiz without penalty during the trimester. However, if a student was absent for an announced quiz or test, she or he must use that test or quiz as the dropped grade. We strongly believed that students must realize that repeated absences must inevitably affect their grade. We agreed that if a student recognized a conflict with a test or quiz date, arrangements could be made to take the test *earlier*—but *not after* the scheduled class administration.

Ms. D said that an AVID teacher approached her and said that this policy conflicted with the California Education Code. She related that all of the AVID teachers believed that students should be allowed to take as many make-ups as they required whenever they were absent. I told Ms. D that she should request the citation in the Ed Code. I did say that once we got the citation, if we found that we were out of compliance, then we would have to decide how to address this part of our protocol.

I also said that I thought most students would be opposed to abandoning the make-up practice. An alternative might be to count the final benchmark in the place of the missed quiz or test for grading purposes. This option would still be advantageous to students because: (1) the benchmark test does not assess the specific chapter content to the degree that the chapter test or sectional quiz does; and (2) since the benchmark test is given at the end of the trimester, the student has more time to study the content. I repeated the suggestion that we plan to meet with the AVID faculty so that our objectives can be explained in a structured and professional environment.

❖ ❖ ❖

Commentary

KATRINE CZAJKOWSKI

I am a high school teacher. Credentialed in English, mathematics, and social studies, I have taught most levels of each discipline in grades 9 through 12 during my 16-year career as a public school teacher working within five miles of the United States–Mexico border. Dismayed by my experience teaching mathematics, I pursued a doctorate to try to understand why I was leaving school daily with the sickening feeling that I was hurting innocent people. I'd careened through quadratic equations four times in one day, and I felt like my hit-and-run teaching had left far too many casualties lying by the roadside. I emerged from my studies with the conclusion that high school mathematics is a lot more about access to opportunity than about symbolic manipulation. At schools where students' experiences with mathematics are particularly terrible, math instruction becomes just one gauntlet through which students must pass. Few emerge intact at the other end.

As I read Barbara Wells's notes and compared them to my past experiences and current reality teaching at a Title I school in year three of Program Improvement, three major issues emerged.

1. What is a "good" math teacher? Much of Barbara's observations focus on the quality of instruction she sees when visiting classrooms. While curriculum, assessments, and resources all contribute to student success, teacher quality far outweighs any other factor. Barbara's comments suggest that the best math teachers have the following qualities.

They care for students as human beings, not inanimate objects.
- They create conditions where students interact, participate, challenge, and defend ideas.
- They acknowledge and address students' life experiences, including their language skills; capitalize on opportunities to discuss etymology, multiple meanings of words, and vocabulary in context.
- They model and value curiosity and inquiry (not trivial personalization of problems).

They have content knowledge.
- They create tasks requiring higher-level thinking.
- They connect discrete skills to a "big idea" or theme.

They have pedagogical expertise.
- They scaffold tasks so students can enter and leave them at various levels.
- They differentiate instruction so students with varying proficiency can learn.
- They make thinking and reasoning visible to students.

They function as collaborators.
- These teachers contribute to the development of a professional learning community.

2. *The dominant practice of treating students like objects, not people, is a symptom of the low expectations that cripple opportunities for many marginalized students.* At Coastline High School, low expectations and a system based on the expectation of failure (rather than success) are illustrated by the following attributes:

- *Low standards* for student behavior (widespread, distracting eating and drinking in classrooms; teachers' aides who do not represent scholarship)
- Failure of the school and individuals to attend to *basics required for learning* (not planning in advance to secure enough Algebra I books; teacher knowingly using a whiteboard pen that does not work)
- *Pegging course pacing to the slowest students* (requiring present students to wait for absentees before moving ahead in the unit)
- *Absence of probing or higher-level questions* (teachers who do not ask challenging questions, sticking to low-level questions they know students can answer)

· *Dominance of low-level tasks* (use of a T-chart for graphing in Algebra II; lack of conceptual basis for combining integers)

The teachers expressed concern about the "fairness" of including certain test items on benchmark exams when those problems had never been presented to students. This concern evokes the somewhat ironic question of what is considered "fair" at Coastline High. Despite Barbara's tireless efforts to shift the paradigm of the mathematics department and program to a competency-based system, teachers were unable or unwilling to grapple with the notion of "competence." Teachers did not consider these questions:

· How is "competency" defined? For what skills? To what degree?

· How is "competency" measured? With what means? How often? By or for whom?

· Are multiple sources of information used to gauge "competency"?

· What alternatives could we find, develop, or implement to make possible greater achievement of "competency"? How do we give students a second chance to demonstrate skills?

So what is more "fair" to the students at Coastline High: excluding items from a test if students have not already seen them or lowering expectations to the point that students stay mired in the La Brea Tar Pits of low achievement? Who, besides Barbara, is asking those questions?

3. Why are the leadership and work of an external coach like Barbara not provided by someone inside Coastline High School? Could or would a teacher in the math department emerge as a leader of peers with all the qualities needed to persevere, innovate, and collaborate on behalf of students? Does one exist at Coastline? Who? Could it be Ms. D? Clearly, Barbara's comments suggest that this teacher comes closest to what she envisions a good teacher to be, but can Ms. D be a teacher leader? The following reflections illustrate the importance of teacher leadership.

Why are teacher leaders so important in places like Coastline High School?

"Professional development" of teachers is not an experience limited to a summer workshop or orientation. It is an ongoing process. It requires praxis and constant reflection, preferably in a collaborative environment. To grow as a teacher requires taking risks and learning from mistakes. It requires trying things with students and then adjusting for the future. None of this can happen away from the classroom, and few teachers can engage in this kind of activity alone, without guidance, support, or simple feedback. Teaching in most schools, particularly those with myriad challenges, is an isolating activity where, too often, survival becomes one's goal. Frequently, students are objectified before teachers become ossified . . . and then we begin to understand what is happening to Mr. F, who becomes the department chair.

Ownership of the change process, or at least buy-in, requires teacher leadership.

On at least two occasions, Barbara provided examples of where teachers failed to follow through on their commitments to the year's program. When nobody referred to "location" in the context of the coordinate plane, it became clear that teachers had not internalized the concept that they had been so vocal about during the summer training. Whose idea was that, anyway? Whose vision drives changes in the mathematics program at Coastline? Who has an interest in the outcomes? Who has ownership of initiatives, materials, programs, or services? Whose homework center are kids refusing to attend? Who works there? Who hires the tutors? Who makes the decisions? Who controls the money? To what degree are individual teachers invested in the challenge of shifting the math department's paradigm?

There is little incentive to change unless someone from within challenges these dominant beliefs.

Leadership by a teacher who is actually "walking in the shoes" of her or his colleagues lends a different kind of voice to the dialogue on change. The credibility of classroom teaching speaks loudly to fellow teachers. People who use the present tense when discussing curriculum, management, or assessment are much harder to ignore than people using the conditional tense. Somehow teachers cannot escape the face of a colleague they encounter daily; they cannot ignore comments at meetings or workshops. In the most powerful case, teachers cannot ignore arguments supported by student work produced in a colleague's classroom.

The trick is using credibility as a classroom teacher to make change happen . . . and avoid decapitation along the way. The problem, of course, with being a teacher leader among colleagues is that it is very difficult to be a "prophet in one's own land." Now if any teacher considers her or himself a prophet, we have a problem. The best teachers are humble, constantly aware of how much is yet to be learned. But colleagues can be unethical, threatened, backbiting (or stabbing, even), unscrupulous people with whom close relationships are strained or impossible. That is why teacher leaders with significant teaching experience earn the most credibility from their peers. These leaders also have to be excellent classroom teachers. Somehow years of experience working with teenagers thicken one's skin—and the scales deflect blows from grown-ups as well as from younger people. Energetic, positive, idealistic young teachers are eager to effect change. But they are vulnerable. They are not the cannon fodder to exhaust in the name of teacher leadership.

The most important reason to invest in the development of teacher leadership is that there is little real accountability for implementing change without it.

How does one support teacher leadership that advances accountability for change? Integrating procedures that require teachers to share evidence of their students' learning is a big step forward. These steps are necessary: Expect teachers to administer and score common assessments like the benchmark exams. Then do an item analysis that reveals areas where students did relatively well and where they did poorly. Sort the results by teacher, by class period. Publish this information to teachers. Provide highly structured (and non-administrator-supervised) opportunities for dialogue around the data. Who leads this work? If a teacher is responsible, a measure of internal accountability is assured. It is a lot harder to give lip service to a colleague than it is to even the most highly esteemed outside expert. In my experience working in schools like Coastline High, teacher leadership of efforts like those I have described is the single most important factor in making change "real."

Barbara Wells is a singular educator and role model for people in all segments of education. She is a light in the darkness of mathematics education, someone who believes that positive change is always possible. She recognizes the magnitude of the challenges involved in changing how schools work, not to mention the values that lay the foundation for those systems. She is a tireless advocate for equity, someone who really believes in the potential of human beings.

Simply put, Barbara Wells has attempted to do for the teachers at Coastline High School what a great teacher does for her students. This effort is what makes her singular in this discipline; she is a consummate teacher in the best sense of the word. The power of such individuals is tremendous and, like a great teacher, her voice lingers in a room long after she has left it.

What do the classrooms at Coastline High sound like when the day is done? Whose voice lingers there? Any?

Unless teachers at Coastline High School become leaders of changing their own practice, Barbara's voice will fade into memory, teachers' voices will never be audible, and the silence of disinterest, inaction, and doomed students will prevail.

Women of Color Leading Schools

The Journey of Three Principals

Few would argue about the important role principals play in leading our public schools. This case study attempts to uncover issues related to principalship through the voices of three dynamic women of color who are and have been school leaders. We were interested in exploring if women, and women of color in particular, face unique challenges in assuming leadership roles in secondary schools.

Rather than finding a principal who might represent women of color and who had the time to write a case study, we arranged for three leaders to come together and discuss their experiences. We recorded and later edited the conversation so that we could use their words to take us on this journey, revealing what it means to be a woman of color leading a school, and in the case of two of the women, assuming leadership roles at the district level as well.

Leading a school requires a wide range of knowledge, skills, and dispositions, as well as the ability to assume multiple roles at any given time—an instructional leader, visionary, budget expert, mother/father, counselor, and disciplinarian. Current research literature presents many definitions of educational leadership, but someone once defined leadership as taking responsibility for what is important to you. These three educational leaders exemplify this definition. Their deep sense of commitment to their students and to ensuring achievement, equality, and access to a rigorous and engaging education resonates throughout this dialogue.

Principals

Lynn Haines Dodd was principal of two newly established small secondary schools at the McClymonds Educational Complex in West Oakland. She is a 20-year veteran in the Oakland Unified School District. She has taught at all levels, served as a principal at both middle and high schools, and has been a district-level administrator. She currently works for The College Board.

Adriana McNally is Director of School Services in the Los Angeles Unified School District, Local District 7. She has served as principal at both Morningside and Inglewood High Schools, as well as in the district office of Inglewood Unified School District.

Yolanda Valdez is principal of Dinuba High School in the central San Joaquin Valley. She has been an administrator for ten years—four years at Orosi High School as dean of students, two years at Dinuba High School as assistant principal, and four years as principal at Dinuba Middle School.

Interviewers

Alice Kawazoe–CAPP Consultant

Nina Moore–University of California, Office of the President; CAPP Consultant

❖ ❖ ❖

BECOMING A PRINCIPAL

KAWAZOE: *What prompted you to become a high school principal? How did you become a principal?*

VALDEZ: Since high school I wanted to be an administrator, but I never thought I would be a high school administrator. I was very driven. It all started with a migrant counselor in high school who took several of us under his wing and made us believe that we could have the world.

KAWAZOE: *You were a migrant student?*

VALDEZ: Yes, I was, but I grew up mostly in Orosi. My first administrative experience was at Orosi High School as dean of students. Then I was an assistant principal at Dinuba High School. I was principal of Dinuba Middle School, and last year I became principal at Dinuba High School. My superintendent really felt I could do the job. We were going through a transition. The superintendent wanted to appoint me, but I turned down the appointment. I wanted him to open it up, and I wasn't sure I wanted the position. And I wanted teachers to have a say in the selection process. The superintendent left before I began as principal, and the personnel director became the new superintendent. I've worked harder in this job than in anything I've ever done.

KAWAZOE: *You're the first woman principal at Dinuba High?*

VALDEZ: Yes, I'm first the woman principal, and the school is 100 years old. And I'm the first Hispanic. I was the first Hispanic woman principal at the middle school, too.

MOORE: *Amazing in a community that's about 80% Hispanic.*

MCNALLY: I came up through the ranks. I was working on a Pupil Personnel Services credential, and an administrator said, "Why are you doing this? It's a lateral move." But I really wanted to be a counselor. I'm a good listener. Like Yolanda, I never wanted to be appointed to anything. I taught Spanish in high school. One assistant principal said that they needed a counselor, so that got me thinking. I was a teacher for eight years and a counselor for six years. I went into ROP and was a counselor and involved in state initiatives. I realized I could effectuate change. I went to the Los Angeles County Office of Education and came back to Inglewood as assistant principal at Monroe Middle School.

Middle school is a different experience. I remember saying, "If I ever get out of this, I will do everything right." But my middle school experience was wonderful because I had a great principal. I learned team effort and collaboration from that gentleman. We transformed that school. I was approached by the superintendent to apply for the position of principal of Morningside High School. The interview process was very rigorous. On the first day there were three rounds of videotaped interviews—eight hours. The second day was the interview with experts.

When I became principal, I thought, "Oh, my, oh, me, what have I done?" I was principal of Morningside for seven years. After the first year it was clear what the vision of the school was. People were tired of being dumped on. Then I went to Inglewood High School. I now work in L.A. Unified supervising principals. I find my experience as principal helpful in my current work.

My supervisors have always prodded me. One supervisor told me, "You are wasting your time. You can help students from a different chair." She gave me quasi-administrative tasks. The superintendent pushed me to higher ground. He was not interested in discussions of problems. "Okay, what's your solution?" he'd ask. Now I've come full circle. I tell my young principals, "It's important to take steps." I have appreciated the journey.

KAWAZOE: *It's interesting that both of you were prodded and supported in directions that you might not have taken.*

MCNALLY: I'd probably still be a counselor. I love working with students. I was not just the counselor to change classes; I counseled.

KAWAZOE: *Do you miss that in your position now?*

MCNALLY: I still use it. I have two very novice principals who need counseling. Sometimes I'm called upon to run meetings for student leaders and parents who really just need advice and help.

VALDEZ: I desperately miss it. I loved my middle school experience. I had more time to interact with students. I was out there every day and after school. My students from middle school are in every class at the high school. They say, "Mrs. Valdez, we don't see you anymore." The good thing is that they know me. I feel connections, and they know they can come to me.

MCNALLY: In Inglewood, the elementary and middle schools are all on the same plot of land. The high school has 52 acres, so you can imagine how big it is. When ninth graders came in from the middle school, the students said, "(Gasp), Ms. McNally, you again!" I have seen the same students in sixth, seventh, and eighth grades and through twelfth grade. "Remember me?" they asked. "Yes, of course, I remember you."

DODD: I was reflecting on the first two questions—I never even thought I would be in education. I didn't enjoy school as a student. Somebody out there saw something in me that I didn't recognize and pushed me into education at a very early age.

VALDEZ: I bet you can really connect with those students now.

DODD: I just dreaded going to school. At home I heard, "You are not going to lie in bed until 12:00; you are going to school." But to have individuals who were not able to tap into my learning style, and to move into a system that had and still has a lot of racial overtones that keep minority students from graduating from high school, frustrated me. So, a lot of the time I was angry and upset. A librarian saw something in me that made me at least think about education. I did not go into college as a matriculated student. I was working with preschoolers and going to Hunter College in Bronx in the evening. You talk about a learning curve! For five years I was a classroom teacher and moved rapidly into administration, directing a Montessori school. It was on-the-ground training. I was still in school trying to get a B.A. Something innate in me said education was where I was meant to be. But I saw administration as part of a bureaucratic system, and I resisted it.

KAWAZOE: *How did you get from the South Bronx to Oakland?*

DODD: I was born in Berkeley. My family moved to South Bronx when I was four. Elementary school was tough. In junior high I fought every day. Walton High School was an all-girls high school by Hunter College. Bronx High School of Science was for the nerdies. At the upper end was DeWitt Clinton, the all-boys school. I loved art and dance, where I flourished. But you were pigeonholed to learn and respond a certain way, and creativity only occurred in elective classes. I became very arrogant, militant—just daring someone to say something to me. I was following in my grandmother's footsteps. She came from the south and always said, "You must claim a piece of land. If you don't claim that land, then somebody else will claim it for you, and then you will always be a slave. So you claim the land and move forward and the land begins to grow by acreage." For me to go from the South Bronx to McClymonds High School has been a journey. Now I look at some of the things my students are going through, and I know I had that same experience. It's just like 40 years ago. The only thing that has changed is that we have gotten older, but the situations are pretty much mirrored.

KAWAZOE: *What brought you back to Oakland and working with high school students?*

DODD: I applied for an educational director position at Children's Hospital. I had just gotten married and was coming home to my mom's family. My position was cut because of Proposition 13. Then I ran a program with the National Council of Negro Women, Operation Sisters United, for 24 months, working with girls 11 to 16 years of age. It was stressful. My hair started falling out; my toenails hurt. I worked with 175 young women. They were put out of the house, abused; I got calls late at night.

Mary Lou Dupree from the Oakland Unified School District called every day for two months. Finally, I went to Santa Fe Elementary School with a fourth to sixth grade special education class—young men who had been in about 25 to 30 elementary schools. The assistant, little Gracie Robinson, about 4 feet 10 inches, said, "If you stay, you'll be their ninth substitute teacher." I said to the students, "You have to get through this program, or you're going out of here on a slab." They wanted to know what a slab was. I said, "In a pine box because I'll kill every single one of you." I stayed there for four years. I decertified each of them out of special education. The same thing had happened to me. When I became rebellious because of a racial incident, they said I was not capable of learning anymore. At the elementary level, if children don't feel connected, they automatically shut down.

PIGEONHOLING STUDENTS

VALDEZ: All throughout the educational system, we talk about reform, but it's all about whether the kids feel connected to the people at the school.

MCNALLY: Kids are aware of being labeled. I recall an incident at school that was blown out of proportion. The superintendent called a meeting of student leaders, not necessarily the academic leaders, just 30 to 35 young people. I got all boys in my group. One boy was astonished that I knew his name. I asked to hear from him. He said, "Why? Everybody automatically assumes that I'm not going anywhere, that I can't do anything, that all I want to do is fight. Frankly, I think this is a waste of time." That got our discussion going. Over-identification of African American males in special education—that's a widespread problem. They are intelligent, but because no one has heard them, they tend to strike out a lot and get in trouble.

DODD: Because no one has taught them.

MCNALLY: That's right. They get in trouble in third grade, and we get them in ninth grade. I said to one kid, "Why are you in this class?" He said to me, "Why don't you ask the psychologist." Good answer. We were looking at the CAHSEE data, and we noticed that there were special education youngsters who were getting fairly high scores in both English and math. I agree with Lynn about pigeonholing, because we think there is a certain place some students should occupy.

VALDEZ: A lot of it has to do with the educational system because, as you said, I was made to sit down, look forward, and do the work, and that's really the way high schools are set up.

MCNALLY: How sad . . .

MOORE: *How do you help your teachers to not do that because there's so much pigeonholing that happens? Do you have a strategy or do you just keep talking about it?*

VALDEZ: When I started out at Dinuba High School, in my opening speech I began with the iceberg metaphor: You only see this much, but look how much you don't see, and I shared some of my experiences. Before my senior year in high school, a counselor called me in and said, "You got a C- in your Comp. Lit. class. You can't go on into college prep in your senior year." I explained that I was working 30 hours at two jobs, one in the office, and then I went to KFC. I said to her, "Okay, go ahead and give me Business English. I'm going to go to college anyway." I shared some of those experiences about how much we don't know about students and about labeling and what that does to a child.

One thing we tried to do last year was really try to push English-language development (ELD) students because they don't have the luxury of time. They need to be in the regular program as soon as they feel they can do the work, even though our system says they shouldn't be there. Sometimes we have to skip some steps. We had a bit of an uproar with some teachers, and one of my brave English teachers said, "The ELD kids are not progressing as I would like them to progress." So, we got the ELD students together for lunch to find out what they thought they needed. I bought pizza. They said, "We need more help, more practice, more examples, more checking on us." The students shared all this with her. But it took a very brave teacher to want to hear from the students. It helped that I spoke Spanish to them, and they felt comfortable to be able to say what they wanted to say. Those candid conversations need to happen for the system to improve.

MCNALLY: I've always been visible in the classroom. I carved out time to go in and then give feedback. I put into place what I called Power

Wednesdays at Morningside—the opportunity for teachers to share and collaborate about student work and best practices. It happened, not after school when they were tired and didn't want to go to staff development, but during the school day. You manipulate your budget so you can provide quality substitutes, not subs from outside, but take someone who has a second period conference period, pay her per diem to take over a class. That gives teachers the feeling that someone cares. Teaching is the only profession where we don't necessarily continuously upgrade our skills, like doctors or lawyers, but we continue to do the same thing the same way and expect different results.

KAWAZOE: *That's a definition of insanity.*

MCNALLY: Right. It started small, and once teachers started talking about how powerful it was, other departments wanted to join. We started with English and social studies. It was like "Mrs. McNally, how come we can't do that?" "Well, you can. I just need to know that you're interested." So something very small took off. Basically, they were looking at data, looking at a strategy that worked with a particular teacher, and that teacher would share how he or she got the kids to do well. Secondary teachers think they're specialists; everyone's in their own cubbyhole. But everyone was given a chance to share with another specialist how something could be done better. I used to say to them, "You need to work smarter, not harder. You're working too hard. Once you get the idea, you're going to work smart. You're going to feel much better about these kids; they're not going to bother you as much."

The second thing is that the kids are not supposed to be harassing you. You're supposed to harass the kids—in a positive way—in that you have so much going on for them that they don't have the time to think about not doing it. They'll want to get to your class. In small ways if you provide the incentive for teachers to work together, collaborate, listen to each other, and look at each other, you're going to find less of the "Oh, the kid is the problem." They even shared what to do with a particular group of kids; they were pairing up, working in groups—all from that two hours they had every other Wednesday. It's expensive, but it's a matter of sitting with your Site Council to carve out so many hours and so many dollars for this. You'd be surprised the buy-in that we got from the Site Council.

DODD: I found in special education that young people didn't have a voice. When I was asked to move into a program specialist position, I was very clear—if I do this, I only want to work at the secondary level. I could see in the elementary students' IEPs that they never had an opportunity to help plan the course of action that would affect them, both academically and behaviorally. So when I moved into the secondary arena, a colleague and I decided there must be a way to have youth help plan a course of action to eliminate the deficiencies that everyone said they had. At that point it didn't matter if you were special ed or regular ed; somebody had to be carving a pathway to success for you with your input. That's how we got teachers to change. Educators were constantly saying, "You have to learn 25 Dolch words." When they reached the last word, they would go back and start over. How can you justify constantly creating documents that have a human being attached to them where you are not elevating the expectations? Is that your level of teaching competency? Can't you teach beyond this low level? If that's the case, then we don't need you here. And so, you need to go someplace else.

CREATING CHANGE AND USING DATA

KAWAZOE: *How do you create the capacity for change? A lot of school districts are undergoing change, structural change, creating small learning communities, schools within schools, and academies. But what you're talking about is creating change in teaching.*

VALDEZ: In the four years I was at the middle school, I saw the most improvement with collaboration. Now, the school has mandated training. But at the time all I wanted them to do was delineate their pacing calendars for the year so they could all stay on track, and students would have the same program. I also wanted them to learn their curriculum. Too often I found everything still in the shrink-wrap. I also got substitutes, so teachers could have a full-day training once a month, sometimes twice a month. They sat down as core teachers and planned their calendars. They really learned a lot: scoring student writing, selecting benchmarks, seeing how close they were in their scoring—all of that really worked.

MCNALLY: We tested the kids to death, and we wore the teachers out—packaging the information, supervising, and proctoring. But the feedback they were getting was just a list of kids—regular ed, special ed. In my current position I have a superintendent who says that no instruction takes place unless you're looking at data. What is it that you want the kids to go away with? What strategies are you putting in place? She holds me accountable, and I hold my principals accountable.

When I walk into the classrooms, say an AP class, and I don't see anything happening, I want to know from that principal, "What have you done to assist teachers teaching the AP class? Have they had training?" Most of the time the answer is "No." Well, then, that teacher shouldn't be teaching AP; I don't care what the contract says. You'd be surprised how teachers come on board because they want the training.

And we plaster the walls with the data. What do the data mean? If we're here and we took three little baby steps, how did we get there? We take it back to departments, and every other Tuesday we're going to give you information. I'll come around to groups, and I'll answer questions and so will my assistant principal. To sit there with 88 people looking at me, and I'm giving them something they can read, is a waste of time; whereas, if we plan in advance, we can give them something to work on based on data. For example, we're testing science this year. How do we get ready for that? It's not just science, but it's science and English-language arts because students have to read. That's where what I call the specialist nonsense comes in. You may be a biology teacher, but if students can't read the book, you need to get the strategies that will help them unlock the codes for reading the book.

KAWAZOE: *What help or guidance did you give your staff in terms of how they look at data?*

MCNALLY: Data have to be presented in a relevant way. If we're looking at data that say we're less than proficient, and our goal is proficiency, then I would ask, "What do we need to do to get proficient?" We might brainstorm things that we thought were positive and things we thought were challenges. Then we prioritize. In groups we might ask, "What do we need to do to move our kids?" One item might be resources. I need to know if my teachers have textbooks, room, facilities, and technology. In Los Angeles each student gets two books—a book to take home and a book that stays in the class as a result of the Williams lawsuit settlement. I need to know as an administrator if there are enough books. Do I have a system in place to make sure that enough books remain in class? Am I timely enough in getting replacements? These are operational things. Unless you have a functional operational system and teachers' needs are met, good teaching is less likely to happen.

DODD: I like to talk about the word "reform." It sounds to me like a penitentiary. We're talking about reforming the whole bureaucratic system that has not been a fair system for minority students. You look at the statistics: more minority students have been eliminated from access to education, so when we're reforming an environment, what are we really restructuring? We've got to have a plan. But a crucial part has been forgotten, and that is when we restructure, we always say we are reforming academically. We leave out all those other pieces that make a child. We never think about our students' life circumstances. How do we address the health issues that are going to have a definite impact on students? The system does not look at individuals; it looks at how the whole school is moving without taking into account everything that affects students' performance. We have to look at the whole system, but keep in mind the individual student.

MCNALLY: That's your rebellion.

DODD: I've always functioned well in urban environments with the roughest and toughest students. It just seems like that's the energy that gets me up in the morning. As the leader of the school, my primary purpose is to advocate for those young people and to bring to the table the educators so that they can understand more than the academics.

MCNALLY: Can I put a label on that? It's awareness. I think the awareness piece is missing in all the literature and research about involving community.

VALDEZ: Or ignored.

MCNALLY: I can involve a community all I want, but I must bring awareness to the community of what my children's needs are, and what we need to do to get from point A to point B, and then get the commitment not to change into another bureaucratic nightmare, but to work with us within the system that we have created so we can move these young people along.

DODD: I like to think of being a change agent—that we are the ones who have the power to negotiate, to come out with a win-win situation about what's happening in that classroom and what's happening with that young person, and making sure that the win-win is always for that young person. If that is under the heading of the principal, then fine, but it is an area I struggle with and that I see missing in so many schools. Districts don't have that power. That power exists at the school site, where an individual can take what they have and move the whole community fast-forward into a win-win situation for both students and teachers.

MCNALLY: Right!

VALDEZ: I wanted to add something about data. Last year we gave staff data, but then we provided them with probing questions: How are the students in your department doing overall? How is each demographic group doing, and how are they doing on each subtest? How does your pacing calendar reflect those changes? Because if the results on one subtest are so much lower than the others, and you're only spending two days on that standard, then what are you going to do differently? They're doing the work; you're monitoring, but if you don't give them those questions and just say, "Here's the data," they're lost. In middle school before we had a data management program, I had the teachers do it by hand. I actually had every instructional assistant, every secretary, help out right before school began, and I had data for every six-week test for each teacher copied and given to them as they walked in on the first day of school. That was quite a chore. But now the computer program does everything for you. Teachers do a spreadsheet that shows how their whole class performed on a subtest. They not only learned how to use Excel, but they learned what those test scores meant and where the cutoffs were. It was really telling. We spend a whole day on that.

DODD: If you're asking a teacher to look at student performance, and that data reflect the job they did in the classroom, then the data need to be presented in a meaningful way. On several occasions at the high school, we've had big resistance if the data came from the central office. It was not user-friendly information. We've used an outside resource, too, to make sure that the data were presented in a useful, understandable way, so that the teachers could take that information and hopefully use it in transforming teaching practices. But I think the resistance at the high school goes back to what we said earlier: the mentality that they are the specialists; they are the gurus of that particular subject.

VALDEZ: Let me tell you what my English department said when we pulled those kids out of ELD. "We are the English teachers. Why aren't you listening to us?" I looked at every one of those kids' grades. They all passed, and I would check the support class periodically to see if they were succeeding. I'm positive they made our AYP (Adequate

Yearly Progress) for us. That big chunk of students we moved up were those who received the standards-based teaching, and that really boosted our AYP.

MCNALLY: In elementary schools when test scores come back, they're grouped by grade level, and the teachers don't like that, right? So, one of the things I did the first year—and they were all arguing about it— was to list the data by the individual English teacher and math teacher, rather than by grade level or course. That brought about so much change and so many antennas going up, because I could say, "You taught these kids. Let's look at these scores." It's all about ownership. We needed to create that little pool of ownership because they very easily could say, "Well, I got them from Lynn this way." Then I could say, "Well, you've had them for a whole year; you got them in September. We don't test until May, so what did you do?" My thing for teachers used to be, "Turn the page."

DODD: Because our school was so small, it was very obvious who the teacher was. For example, we only had one person teaching tenth-grade English.

MCNALLY: It was an eye-opener. Elementary schools go through it all the time. But in secondary we hide behind the umbrella of no one taking ownership. So I created that ownership for them. When we looked at the data, it was silent. We were not picking on anyone. We just put the data up on big chart paper, and we walked around. I had some guiding questions, so they could take notes.

It's very important for the principal, the educational leader, to know, understand, and be able to interpret data. To me that's crucial. If you're giving out information, and you can't interpret it, then you've lost the respect of that staff or it becomes busy work. A Cal State Fullerton professor stressed the importance of tracing the growth of the same group of kids from grade to grade. Light bulbs went on because everyone thought we were looking at just this year. No! We needed to see if we moved the kids from here to there—the same kids. We're not talking about a different set of kids. Then we can start talking about what strategies to use. As Lynn says, you are the only person teaching them, "So whatcha gonna do?"

KAWAZOE: *What was the reaction in your school?*

MCNALLY: The first year I heard a lot of grumbling. But gradually as you start doing the work, the people who always have an excuse for everything quiet down because the rest of their peers are saying, "We've got to figure this out." How does math influence the science classroom? How does English influence social studies? How does all of this affect life skills?

VALDEZ: The data management program allows you to pull out the information by teacher. So teachers can have their students' CST scores when they walk in the classroom and will have their scores when they walk out of the classroom. Then they own it. Last year we did the training, but people were leery about technology, and they really didn't get into it. Now I'm actually handing them the information, and part of collaboration time will be spent reviewing their own classes' data and then reviewing the department data and disaggregating it. Measures allows them to do all of those things.

DODD: About five years ago, we were classified as an Immediate Intervention/Underperforming School Program (II/USP) school. It was my second year being principal of McClymonds High School, and our external evaluator came in. My first year as principal I was very quiet. I just did my walk-arounds. "You know, she doesn't really want to be here," people would say. I did want to be there, but they knew that I had an agreement with the superintendent that if I didn't want to stay at the school, I could go back to my former school. I would stay for six months, and then I could leave. After about the first six weeks, I knew I wasn't going anyplace. I'm going into my seventh year now.

When we finally looked at the data, people began to understand that not everybody was going to be at the school the next year, but the teachers didn't know how that was going to play out. They were very aware that changes were going to happen. The external evaluator came in, and we were also going to have a Western Association of Schools and Colleges (WASC) accreditation that year. We could have delayed the WASC, but I decided to go through with it. I needed to hear about what was going on. I needed to have outside individuals come in and validate what my gut was feeling. So we had the infor-mation from the WASC self-study, and then the evaluator assessed our strengths and our challenges. We took the data from a four-year period. Nobody at that school had ever seen the big picture. What they were used to seeing was what had happened in their classroom, but not how it had impacted the entire educational environment.

It was very clear that students were coming to the high school with deficiencies, but with some real strategic planning, we could take students from a base level and give them some rigor, and they could rise to the challenge. When they came in at the ninth grade, they were pretty much functioning at a low-basic level. But that was not as severe as what happened when they got to the tenth grade; their learning curve went to far-below basic. The growing started again, just a little increment, at the eleventh grade, and at the twelfth grade they were still at a basic level, but they had acquired some skills, so they could still graduate.

Teachers at the tenth grade had become complacent. They were thinking, "They're coming to me at this level, and I don't need to do anything else."

CHANGING TEACHING AND TEACHERS

DODD: McClymonds had more teachers who were incompetent than teachers who were good or master teachers, so the majority of the students unfortunately were with individuals who could not teach.

MCNALLY: We put in place all these intervention programs for the children who are far below and below basic. Unfortunately, often the teachers who are teaching them in the regular program are the same teachers teaching them in the intervention program, and they already have not been successful with these students.

VALDEZ: They're the only ones who apply for the jobs . . .

MCNALLY: Well, that, too, but in some cases it's an issue of seniority. We must become bold and take a risk and say, "No! This cannot continue." These kids need the rigor, and the people who are going to give them the rigor are those master teachers who are doing a good job.

DODD: But if the majority of your teaching population is in a deficit, then all you're doing is recycling through a deficit. If the good teachers are so small in number, only a small percentage of students is going to have a positive learning experience. I had been at McClymonds as an assistant principal—that's a baptism-by-fire story—but it had been ten years since I had gone back in the position of principal, and in those ten years, there had been at least five or six different principals.

I spent the first year just figuring out what was going on. Out of a teaching force of maybe 30, most of whom had been there for some time, none of them had ever been evaluated. Nobody had said to them, "What you're doing is great or what you're doing needs to be improved or what you're doing is so detrimental to students you need to move on." The evaluation process became a major issue with me the second year. At the end of that year, we finally got the report back from the external evaluator, which just mirrored what the WASC report had said: little or no teaching was going on at the school.

VALDEZ: I've noticed in my school that with the junior- and senior-level teachers, seniority is the issue. Those teachers who had been teaching 20 years or more were teaching in a pre-standards-based instructional era. The new teachers, who had recently taken teacher education classes, were familiar with the standards and knew how to standards-plan. They were doing a good job for the most part, and the more tenured teachers were just beginning to learn about standards-based instruction and were fighting it. I had a teacher who had been teaching for 23 years, and she had been teaching the same way the whole time. She thought she was doing standards-based instruction, but really, that was not what is happening. So, the collaboration time is where teachers can see what real standards-based instruction looks like.

DODD: I agree. I was thinking about the question, "What was the most satisfying and what was the most dismaying experience . . . ?" For me that would have been my second year when I was able to say to some of the faculty, "You can't be here," which was very satisfying, considering all the injustices that had gone on with students for years. But the dismaying part was the toll that it takes on you as the administrator, because now you're playing with an adult's life who may have rent or a mortgage or a family. You're saying, "You can't to be here next year." You've got to be very honest and fair in the process. That's great for me, but they've not been dismissed from the district. They're going to go someplace else and continue to do damage. You think, "Oh, goodness, now 150 students at another place are going to experience the damage." You never learn these things at the university or in administrative programs. They don't teach you how to deal with the emotional levels that you are going to go through as the leader. It's not in the textbook; there's no cookie cutter way of doing it.

VALDEZ: My husband and I were talking about what has made us successful, because we've both been promoted through the ranks. He's in private business, and I'm in education, and we say "common sense." So many people don't have the common sense to make those decisions.

MCNALLY: I've got to follow up on what you were saying about evaluation. It really doesn't bother me when you have to make a decision to let someone go because for the whole year you've been trying to guide that person, giving them feedback, being in their classroom, providing a coach. You've done all you can do. There have been warnings along the way. You've given a first "need to improve" notice, and following the contract, you've provided a prescription for improvement. You've given them a second notice. I hear what you are saying in terms of impacting a life, but the most important reason we have are those children. So, if the teachers have shown no improvement the whole year, as the leader, I have to be honest. A few times I've bluntly said, "If you were in any other industry, you'd be gone; go pick up your paycheck."

DODD: I agree, but if you've never had anybody tell you that you were ineffective, and now somebody is telling you—it's hard. The second year I did a massive sweep; I identified 12 people who were going to get transfer notices. I agree with everything you say—if teachers are not performing, they definitely need to move on, after you've given them the opportunity to grow over the course of the year. I saw a complete lack of teaching, and I knew I had to take the school on a corrective path. Sometimes you take the risk, and that's the thing you're not going to find in the textbook.

MCNALLY: Another thing you're not going to find in the textbook is the impact that such action has on the rest of the faculty—the division, the morale. One of the first things I had to do in my very first assignment was forget data. I had to do some team building. One of the teachers had done some work at Johns Hopkins on brain-based research, and we began to delve into character development and its influence on students. We went through three months just charting out our plans. We discussed our influence on the students and on each other, and we learned about our strengths and weaknesses. We all read *What Color Is Your Parachute?* That was one of the most satisfying experiences I've had because people discovered things that they didn't know about themselves. Here we were trying to teach children, and we were just beginning to learn how to and how not to work with others. The teachers were working on the same campus where I had worked for 25 years, but they had never come across the lawn to speak to me because they were in English, and I was in foreign language. We found out that someone had strengths that another could rely on, and our cultural backgrounds showed that we were more alike than different. All those kinds of things became so important.

That was all in my first year. I thought there was no way in the world I was going to get this staff together, with some of them sitting in the back of the room with "make me" looks on their faces. I thought, "I'm going to make you, but I can't make you by just talking." None of them had been evaluated for a while, so a rumble went through the room when I said, "All bets are off; everyone's getting evaluated this year."

I had to be ready, and I thought, "I can't do this alone." I had to build collaboration. As a result of the *What Color Is Your Parachute* activity, they were all still talking. Every day in the staff lounge, you'd hear, "Yeah, man, what color are you? You're more dominant than I am." It was good conversation; they weren't complaining about kids. It was conversation based on their research, and it hit home.

The next year the staff was disappointed because they were ready to continue, but I was gone. And the next principal didn't have that training to take it further. She was honest enough to tell them, "This was Mrs. McNally's work. We'll do it as much as we can, but if it's not broke, we won't fix it." But "Mrs. McNally's work" was just getting them to understand that they were responsible for the 150 lives that came through their door every single day. They had to to help students every day. They could go to the psychologist and pay $150 and get help. These kids didn't have that luxury, and the teachers had a limited time with them. It's not about the teachers; it's about the students.

Those were the hard conversations that I can remember having with staff. One of the other satisfying moments was when I said to the staff, "We're going to host the Academic Decathlon." They thought I was crazy. "We're a football school; we're a basketball school." "Yeah? Well, we're also a brain school" was the thrust of the conversation. We embarked on this journey of hosting 66 other schools at our school. I got everything I needed from the district office in terms of facilities support. They redid our gym. We got things fixed that had been broken for years. We got the community to come out because there were things our district couldn't do. We tapped into local gardeners and our parents who had small businesses. We tapped into home improvement stores and got free paint, rakes, and brooms. We wanted to see our community transform a school. We got green lawns and newly painted buildings and rooms.

I told the student body, "I need volunteers to be docents." "What you talkin' about Mrs. Mac? What's a docent?" They never heard the word. But you should have seen our kids running around in T-shirts, helping. It was the pride. The county invited us to do it a second year. All the schools said it was the best they had ever seen in terms of whole school involvement. I told the kids, "This is like hosting the Olympics." What was most satisfying for me to see was the pride not only of the students, but the teachers, the custodians, and the clerical staff. I said, "I can't pay you, but I need people to be here as runners." People showed up. We had more folks than we needed. Teachers were going into their pockets because we didn't have enough money to buy the T-shirts that said, "Morningside High Docent." So the most satisfying moment I had was coming up with an idea and a vision to transform the school that said it's okay to be good athletically, but it's also good to use that up here (pointing to her head). I used to tell the kids, "The decathlon is academic high jinx. Come with me; let's do this." And they did it.

At one point the fire marshal shut us down. We had too many people. We couldn't get that many people in the gymnasium. We got Hollywood Park to announce it on the freeway marquee, "Superquiz—Show Up." We had parents showing up out of curiosity who would never have come to the school. It just shows what you can do when you marshal a force together. I was there every Saturday of my life for a year, preparing this stuff. But it was okay. It was very satisfying because everybody else showed up. Everybody brought a rake or brush and did gardens and painting. The district couldn't paint. They gave us the gym, but they couldn't do anything else in terms of the fix up that we needed around the school.

It remained that way, even after the decathlon. It remained and flourished. We got a club, a horticulture club, spearheaded by a math teacher. He got his math kids together, and they created gardens all over that school. It just shows you've got to tap into something, bring people along, and they'll take care of it.

SUSTAINING THE WORK

KAWAZOE: *It is really true that Lynn's school, through the years, became a dumping ground, so for her to get the privilege of cleaning house and bringing people's attention to their teaching was a once-in-a-lifetime exercise of power. We talk about low-performing schools, but*

*there are low-performing teachers, too. The superintendent gave her
the opportunity to remove her lowest performing teachers that year;
she wouldn't have that chance again. But what happens to your efforts
after you leave the school?*

MCNALLY: For a while some of it is sustained, and it depends on the
leaders of the place. For the most part, in the first year-and-a-half after
I left, I saw a lot of good things still continuing. But it was mainly
because of the teachers.

The frustration comes when they begin to get leader after leader.
The excitement and hope begin to dwindle. It's disheartening to me
because I know how hard we worked. Our school was transformed
into the school where the district held all the big teacher meetings.
Everything was held there because it was pristine; it was safe. They
used to say to me, "How did you get the grass to grow here?" I said,
"You water it. You take care of it." Is some of that still happening?
To some degree it is, but a lot of it has been lost. I don't want to place
blame, but the blame is in the lack of consistency.

KAWAZOE: *One of our concerns is—when the charismatic leader
leaves, how can improvement at a school be sustained over the long
haul?*

VALDEZ: It's really interesting to me—the middle school had a turn-
around in the four years I was there. We made our API every year; I
really felt we'd built a family. A lot of good things were developing at
the school. And then I left for the high school, and a new leader came
in. Things kind of fell to the wayside to a certain extent. It could be
that they were finding themselves, but it really had to do with the
district-level management. It is the carrier of the full vision, and it
should know what is going on at every school. Perhaps the district
people should have told the incoming leader, "These things are going
really well. Maybe for your first year, don't touch these things," or
something to that effect, something that maintains the staff's and the
school's direction.

I left and came to the high school. The high school wasn't in the
process of being turned around; it was turned around. So unlike the
way I came into the middle school, I had to make sure I sustained
what was already at the high school and not necessarily institute my
own views just because I wanted to institute my own views. Because
I grew up in the district, and I knew that the staff had already gone
through some of these reform activities, my job was to make sure that

teachers sustained and improved the level of instruction. My mission was to continue improving upon what was there. I took on a different role than I did my first year at the middle school. I observed; I listened; I took notes; I sent out surveys to parents, to teachers, and to students.

This year my job is to start implementing the WASC recommendations because last year we went through WASC, which was fantastic for a first-year principal. I really got to learn about the school and know what was happening as we did our self-study.

MCNALLY: Everything I've ever read says that one of the pitfalls of new administrators is that they come in and immediately want to change everything. I learned that a long time ago from this gentleman under whom I was assistant principal. When he came in, the school wasn't in order, but he didn't come in cutting people's heads off. He came in; he took notes; we took notes. We had meetings every afternoon on what had happened. In February or March when we started getting ready for next the year, he called in staff, key administrators, and counselors. We had our plan and went through it. Some people would not be with us the next year, so we had to plan for that. Often when districts lose people or move people and bring someone else in, there's not that sit-down, collaborative discussion about expectations, systems, and needs. The new person comes in, and he or she has to just start swimming.

VALDEZ: With not much direction.

MCNALLY: Right. And unfortunately that person gets blamed for whatever negative thing happens. If he or she does all right, then all kinds of banners go up. But I can remember coming into my new high school and saying, "Oh me, oh my, what have I done?" But I had a superintendent who was very supportive, and he would listen; then he would stop and ask, "OK, what do you want to do? What's your solution?" If you had a solution and you gave it to him, he would say, "Reduce it to writing; give me a plan." If you gave him a plan, he immediately met with his deputy superintendent, and they met with business services, and they had you in the meeting. You could see that you were going to be supported. Not all superintendents are like that. The woman I work for now is like that. She'll say, "Plan. Get with your principal and come up with a plan. Help your principal to formulate a plan. What's your expectation?" Once you give it back to her, she'll take it downtown. I don't think that happens in a lot of districts where new people come in, and they are just expected to swim upstream.

VALDEZ: When I first started at the junior high, I had a whole day of orientation about what the school needed and what I needed to do. There are pros and cons about that. Somewhere in the middle is the truth.

MOORE: *Lynn, I think you got placed a week or two before school started?*

DODD: It was actually the first day of return for administrators. McClymonds is a school that has been constantly on the chopping block for closure. So I approached McClymonds with the perspective of what was best for students. I looked at the historical context and the school's legacy within the community, and I had a private passion and a mission that the students of West Oakland would not have to go someplace else to receive a quality education. I put systems in place that will sustain McClymonds High School, now called the Complex, because it will have the two small high schools and a middle school sharing the same campus.

I wanted to put systems in place so the district could not close the school. We have a health clinic on our property that Children's Hospital operates, and although the clinic is on the school campus, the district does not run it. How could the district say we're closing down the health clinic that is servicing not only the high school students, but will service the middle grades students and in the third year of operation will expand to serve the residents of West Oakland? If they closed the campus, there would be a political backlash. That's the way I've attacked the issue of keeping the school viable: by focusing on the whole child. We put the health clinic on campus, and now we're hiring a fulltime director to manage the youth and family support center. So, we've got another entity that they've got to deal with from the community if they decide to close the school. It's all about providing a comprehensive environment that addresses the needs of the whole child.

Academics are still at the forefront. I hope that we will continue the notion that this is a college-going environment. The goal is for any student who graduates from the Complex to be eligible for UC admission. Whether they decide to go down that path or not is a whole different ball game. I would hope that when I step down, the district will look for someone to carry on that vision and to be ready to deal with community, district, and city issues. It's difficult to find all that in a lot of educators, because they're not willing to tackle it all. But if you come from the perspective I come from, how do you not tackle everything, if you're trying to make sure a system is whole and healthy?

MCNALLY: But the key point is that the district, in making those appointments, needs to know and understand the school's goals, dreams, and vision and find a person who, first of all, is experienced enough to carry on. The replacement is not going to be exactly like the person who left, but it's not about the person; it's about the system and the services that have been put in place. Then the person may have a good chance of providing some positive continuity. Often that does not happen. Second, the sustaining factors, even more than the person coming in, are the teachers, parents, families, and communities that have been developed along the way. In districts and schools that do well, it's not necessarily just because of a principal, but because of a system that the principal managed to put in place and the empowerment everyone has. I have a school like that now. We're losing the principal, but I'm not worried about that school because the administrative staff and faculty are so tight, and they work so collaboratively.

DODD: That's grooming the environment, so that when you leave, something can hold it together.

MCNALLY: Right, right. But the people who will be interviewing candidates must know what it's going to take to continue to get some good results.

BUILDING LEADERSHIP CAPACITY

KAWAZOE: *That touches on the question of how you build leadership capacity at a school.*

VALDEZ: Give them the opportunity to lead.

MOORE: *What kind of skills do you think leaders need?*

DODD: You look at your faculty and your community. One of the things that I wanted to see happen at McClymonds was to expand their voice in the decision-making process. I had the ultimate say-so, but I didn't feel that that was the right way to work with this particular community. We created a leadership team that consisted, for the first two years, of only faculty and classified people. They were hand picked—those who I knew wanted to go through a change process and were committed to a vision of the school and creating a college-going culture.

After the first two years, we expanded the leadership team to include community representatives and students. When students became a part of the leadership team, it took on a whole different element, because it had been a school that did not value youth voice and participation. It took about two years for me to get faculty to the point that they would allow—I use the "allow" because that's the word they used—a student to sit at the table and talk about issues related to academics, school climate, and teaching. The only thing we would not do in the presence of students was talk specifically about a particular teacher. If we were talking in general about the lack of rigorous lessons, some of the students might say, "In biology class we're not getting enough labs." We're not specifically talking about an individual, but rather the content of the class. These discussions began to take the school in a whole different direction because we were listening to what students had to say and wanted. But sometimes you have a group of seasoned educators, with numerous years of teaching under their belts, who don't necessarily value youth voices. Their position is, "You do as I say, not as you want. This is the way it's going to be." The fact is that we were open, and I was forceful enough to say that I would not have it any other way.

I wanted to have community and parent involvement. I wanted to bring partners outside of the school district to create positive momentum. I knew I couldn't do it by myself. That's what I believe is the catalyst for change and that's how I got the leadership team to function. The thing was to open up the power that was within me to say, "I need your input, and I value your voice." What we talked about within the confines of the leadership room was kept there. When we needed to get to the nitty-gritty about teacher performance, the discussion stayed in the room. I built that type of trust and rapport, but many people did not appreciate it, and many people tried to sabotage the process on more than one occasion. But we stayed the course.

VALDEZ: Who would try to sabotage? Was it because students were involved?

DODD: They were the teachers who just didn't want to see change, who wanted to take the school down a path that was self-serving as opposed to constantly having students at the top of the agenda.

VALDEZ: I would have thought you would have given those teachers their walking papers when you had the chance.

DODD: Over the course of seven years, and I don't say this with pride because I don't think it's anything to be proud of, there's been a turn-over of about 20 to 25 teachers out of a staff of 30 that we had to move out. There have been a lot of changes for the good. Some people right now are willing to change, or they will opt to sever the ties at the end of the school year.

MCNALLY: People have to feel that they have a stake in the vision. Vision should not be developed top-down; it has to be developed col-laboratively. Also, it's important to give people specific responsibilities, and as principals, constantly check with them and give them feedback.

VALDEZ: What does that look like? What are some suggestions?

MCNALLY: Teachers and administrators react more positively and want to participate when they feel valued. Many times we work people to death. We almost never say, "Good job, thank you." But we're very quick to speak when something goes wrong. A leader should have good listening skills and empathy. And as Lynn said, we must understand our children's life circumstances and what they are going through. Similarly, none of us leaves our personal issues at the gate when we get out of our cars in the morning, because personal issues are a part of us. As a leader, I have to be sensitive to what's going on with Lynn today. She's usually her wonderful, perky self. Today I've heard her snap at a few kids and two or three staff members. I have to be aware of those things and find time to pull her aside and see what's happening and how I can be of support.

Lynn talked about her clinic. Technically, we have a clinic in each of our schools because we have to be that doctor, that psychologist, that nurse, that person with the empathy who encourages and moves people along. People who are bullies may want things done a certain way. Everybody gets involved except them. When it looks good, they take all the praise, and when it looks bad, they blame everyone around the table—we must tend to them because that's what kills the spirit and creates apathy among faculty and support staff.

When a leader is collaborative, when he or she is open and sets clear expectations and is able to lay out a plan clearly, the leader is more likely to have support for implementation. Support doesn't mean, "Every time you mess up, I'll write you up." It's checking, it's monitoring, it's praising, it's giving direct help, "You did that well, but how about if we try this next time?" It's value added.

When I was at Morningside, I had twin sons who were both in college. One chose to be on the east coast, and one was on the west coast. One played football; the other didn't. During the four years Derek was in New York, my husband and I went almost every weekend to his games. I left Thursday night on the red eye for New York and returned on the red eye for school Monday morning. During that time I never had a doubt that if there were a problem, the school would run successfully, without chaos. Dr. Nash, the superintendent, used to say to me, "McNally, you should credit yourself for that." He always had me talking about Walt Whitman, saying that the sign of a good leader is that you are leaving the wealth of your experience to those left behind.

VALDEZ: Building our vice principals is very important, so that our schools will always be maintained as if we were there. I've worked with administrators who felt very good about leaving me alone as a vice principal and being able to run the school. I learned the most in those situations. I was in my element, a kind of baptism by fire, but it was a great learning experience. I've also worked with administrators who wouldn't give me any responsibility other than discipline, and I didn't want to be "just discipline." I want to be an administrator who really gives feedback to my vice principals, gives them the accolades and credit, and also shares with them, saying, "You might look at this because when you're sitting in my chair (and I know you're going to sit in my chair at some time), this can happen. I tell them stories that have happened to me, so they can learn from my mistakes. It's really helped the administrators that I've worked with.

I've found it much easier at the middle school to build a site-based management team. The first year here at Dinuba High School, I didn't get much feedback from the Leadership Team. After listening to Lynn, I'm going to handpick the people and include students. It's really going to change the dynamics. I want them to question me and ask, "What about this?" I want them to give me feedback. Most of the year when we needed to consider the staff development plan or I asked what they needed, I got very little feedback. I felt like I was alone, leading the school, and that's okay; I can do that because I'm more of a dictator sometimes than not. But getting feedback from the staff was tough this year.

KAWAZOE: *If they came from a culture where they were not accustomed to giving feedback . . .*

VALDEZ: I think that's what it was, and then also they had to get to know the new principal. Although I was their assistant principal, they didn't know me. They had heard how I come in strong to a school so it was a getting-to-know-you period. I'm hoping the second year will be a lot different.

BEING WOMEN OF COLOR

DODD: Providing an opportunity for people to be risk takers and to implement something that they have a passion to do is another way of grooming leaders, whether it's in an administrative capacity or to take on various leadership roles at the school.

Going back to the principalship and women of color. Up until this past school year, I have been the only female in an administrative component of all African American males. Now that's a different dynamic! How do you, an African American female, develop a support system of African American males when one on the team wanted the principalship and didn't get it?

I've gone through interesting years at McClymonds. I was a first-year principal who had two male, African American assistant principals and a female who was retiring. She was there sometimes, and then she wasn't. She was a good person, but she was clearly in the retirement mode. The second year I was given a brand new assistant principal.

VALDEZ: What do you mean "given"?

DODD: He was handpicked by the superintendent and given to me. It was very interesting having to deal with that. But we worked through it, and the person lasted for two years. There's just a certain level of necessary learning, and that learning curve wasn't going anyplace. Nice person, but he was clearly on another path, and he did not want to really learn the grassroots.

It was interesting dealing with three males. Sometimes I would call a colleague and get a male perspective on how to handle situations. Yolanda Peeks from the central office administration was also there for me. Yolanda would just sit there and listen. I would let go of all my frustrations. How do you ask somebody to do something when you know that you're in the position that they wanted to be in? How do you work with this male who did not handle a situation like you wanted him to handle it without damaging his ego? Males are a funny breed out there—especially if a female is giving them directives. How do you delicately, but firmly, say something so that you're not damaging the team's relationship? I always had to look at how I was going to make sure that the team was coming together and putting students at the top of the agenda.

I had to be careful that the men were not feeling that I was just playing to their maleness or not recognizing that their egos were just strong as mine. If I wanted to say something about football because something was not happening appropriately on the football team, how did I make my point when they were the ones who know everything about football? I wanted to present the perspective that the student's action was inappropriate and it had nothing to do with the athletic aspect. We should take him off the team, regardless of whether the team was going to win or lose.

VALDEZ: I know exactly what you're talking about.

DODD: Eventually two of the administrators moved on, and one has stayed with me. It's like a marriage now with this one. We fight every single day. But it's a good, healthy fight now. We've been together so long—seven years at this school and five years at another school.

VALDEZ: You're like an old married couple.

DODD: We're an old married couple, and we act like it, too.

VALDEZ: Will this marriage last?

DODD: It's going to last because there is no threat in terms of position. He's going to retire. What happens to me is another thing, but it's at that level now where we can pretty much say anything we want to say to each other respectfully. I don't have to agree with him, but I do need to get my issues out on the table. It's taken a while to get to that point where the dialogue is comfortable enough that we walk away from the table and still come back the next day, respect each other as administrators, and be friends.

VALDEZ: That was exactly the same with my vice principal. He aspired to have the high school position. I don't think the district's support was there, only because he was green. He is going to be a great principal some day. He and I had a heart-to-heart. Actually, I walked into the same situation at the junior high with a vice principal who had been there for 20 years and had tried for the principalship three or four times. At the high school I told the vice principal what my goals and mission were, and I asked him how I could help him. I gave him opportunities being in front of staff, running staff development, and taking on important responsibilities that really helped me. He felt valued and that I believed in him. Giving him all those opportunities really won him over.

DODD: This past year the tables turned. The male assistant principal was still with me, and we had two new female assistant principals who were being groomed for the principalships of the two new, small high schools.

I was standing in the plaza one day, and a student who has now moved on to the University of Michigan came over and said, "Ms. Dodd, do you like everything that's going on at the campus right now—all this change?" And I said, "Yes." He said, "Well, I don't." I said, "Why not?" He said, "I don't think you need to break up the school into two schools." And I said, "Why?" He said, "'Cause they're not going to do it like you." I said, "I don't want them to do it like me. That's the whole process. We're creating something new." He kind of hurt my feelings to a certain extent when he said, "'Cause you didn't train them well." I said, "What do you mean by that?" He said, "One will collaborate, but she only wants to collaborate on things she wants to collaborate on. The other, when you give her something to do, it's going to take her a year to do it."

Those were the very things I had been struggling with. Wow! "From the mouths of babes." I had to go back and start rethinking some things to put in place to make the change, because the assistant principals were focusing more on making changes in the structure as opposed to learning the operations and all the things we've been talking about.

VALDEZ: That happened, too, to the new principal when we opened a new school. None of the nuts and bolts were worked out with this new young female principal, and it was a nightmare with the community newspaper and parents complaining. Simple things were not in place.

DODD: I wanted them to focus on designing their new schools and making sure that their plans were so tight they would pass board approval. What I ended up doing was taking on all their responsibilities for running the school and doing their planning for their new schools. "Oh, that's not going to be finished on time? Okay, I'll take it and do it to meet the deadline." I wanted to make sure that McClymonds never had the stigma that it couldn't get the job done. But that was a rude awakening for me.

VALDEZ: Great insight, but a great burden.

ADMINISTRATIVE TRAINING PROGRAMS

MOORE: *I'd like to go to the question about administrative credential programs and whether or not they prepared you. You all talk about the way you came in, but none of you mentioned anything about the administrative training program. Given what you've said about building capacity, how did your administrative training program prepare you to lead?*

MCNALLY: I think pedagogically the program at Pepperdine prepared me well for working in systems and teams with a big emphasis on curriculum development and finance, and it utilized real people working in districts. It gave us scenarios, and it also had us find a financial problem in the district (if the district would allow us to), and then analyze the problem and come up with solutions. Working in cohorts was very good because it really helped us understand the collaborative process, and sometimes we would have to take on the role of leader.

It did not prepare me for data collection and analysis and how data drive instruction. It did not prepare me for doing a master schedule or overseeing the development of a master schedule. I got that from having been a counselor and seeing all the dumb stuff that went on. The program dealt a lot with the law and the Education Code, but I really learned about that when I hit the ground running at a school. I needed to check the legality in the big orange book, the Ed. Code.

The program didn't prepare me at all for irate parents. Honest, genuine field work, which was a big part of the Tier I program, really helped, provided it was done correctly. I had an advisor, Dr. Bowick, who was always in my face. David would just show up at my site, and while I was running around, he'd want to know how did that relate to a particular competency. He'd speak to my principal about how I was doing, and then when I got back to the college, he had notes on everything he noticed. If you managed to have supervisors like that, you might touch on some of the things that don't come out in the textbook. But a lot of it is just common sense and heart, a lot of heart.

VALDEZ: For me the program provided a foundation, but everything that the leadership position requires I learned on the job, and by having principals that allowed me to pretty much run the school. Boy, did I learn! Really, an opportunity to shadow administrators—walk with them, a kind of a day-in-your-life—would give people insight as to how to deal with the things that happen day in and day out.

DODD: I would love to take the two evolving administrators at the school through one more year of some really hands-on work. I think they would just shine after that. The program I went through at St. Mary's was a good program, and I appreciate what I learned—but one of the things I clearly remember that they did not teach was how to operate if you were placed in an urban setting that had a very diverse population. It was never, ever mentioned. How do you deal with communities that don't necessarily embrace or value education? How do you keep that community actively involved? How do you get faculty to begin to understand your students' life circumstances? The textbook doesn't prepare you for that. Some programs now train administrators in urban settings, but all programs need to have at least a strand of working with these issues. Even if you don't intend to work in an urban community, future administrators need to see that it's not a cookie-cutter type of student we're getting.

DEALING WITH RACISM

KAWAZOE: *You've been talking a lot today about how to increase strategies for learning, and looking at data, and helping teachers to gain ownership over their students and their achievement. But how do you deal with or work to change the attitudes that perpetuate racism either at your school, at the district level, or in your community?*

VALDEZ: I empower parents. I am so blunt with my parents. I tell my parents, "Hold me accountable." Hold each and every one of my teachers accountable. Let me explain to you how. Almost every meeting I give them a little something. I tell them there are those parents who are on our doorstep, are in the classroom, are asking the teachers questions, and are making sure their kids get the attention. I tell them,

"You need to be those parents." I say this to my English Language Advisory Committee parents. I say this to my Parent Academy, and to those parents who usually don't have a voice.

In junior high what really made a big difference was when we offered a grant-funded Parent Institute for Quality Education. When the grant ended, we created our own academy, paralleling what we had learned from the parent institute. All the parents who graduated from that parent academy are involved at my school. That is really rewarding. They are parents who would usually not be involved.

Building that type of communication and leadership with the teachers involves just being straightforward. I met with 15 English teachers on the subject of ELD students and said, "These kids do not have the luxury of time. What can we do now with what we have to help these kids through?" Then we had to build bridges with the ELD department so that the transition into "regular classes" in the English department was much smoother.

DODD: I've dealt with the issue of racism on a one-to-one basis. What I'm hoping will eventually happen is that colleagues address the issue and not necessarily say, "Oh, Ms. Dodd is going to handle it" if they see or hear inappropriate comments or language on campus. They always know that somebody is going to handle it, but they have to feel confident enough to challenge people, especially their colleagues, their peers, on racial issues. But that's a hard subject.

VALDEZ: Having low expectations of students is a kind of racism. I'm working with my ELD teachers and moving them forward because sometimes they baby these kids and don't challenge them. I'm also working with the English department and working with students. I go into classes and repeatedly give students pep talks. I tell them my story and tell them what they need to do to succeed. We have student meetings and assemblies where successful students relate their stories and inspire others. Several kids have come to me and said, "Mrs. Valdez, I'm going to be the one who's going to be speaking up there next year." So, we need to let them know continually that their interests are foremost in our minds. But they need to help themselves, too. They need to go into the counselor's office and demand college prep classes; they need to ask questions and request more explanations from teachers if they don't understand; they need to come to the principal when they have an issue. They need to be empowered.

MCNALLY: Lynn says she deals with racism on a one-on-one basis, and I do, too. Sometimes issues and rumors fly, and things get out of hand. That's when I'll step in. I always call it the elephant in the room and say we need to deal with the elephant and speak from facts. I will let them know what the situation is because they all know pieces of it anyway. But I will meet separately with the person or persons who may be behind whatever it is. You have to be careful even when you meet with them separately, because the first thing they say is you're violating their freedom of speech.

VALDEZ: Or you're a person of color.

MCNALLY: Right. I always say to them to try to put themselves in the situation. I like to use stories and incidents from history to make a point about discrimination or bias or sexism.

I remember saying very directly to one man, "Just what is it you think you're doing?" because he was so bad. He was blatant about it. I was never so embarrassed because we had visitors. This math teacher was trying to teach students the difference between deca and hexa, and he used a small figure of a female for deca, and a big, hefty man with muscles for hexa and made some very inappropriate remarks. I almost died. But it wasn't the first time. We had received comments from students that Mr. So&So was always making sexist and racist remarks, so I had to deal with it very severely.

I deal with racism on a case-by-case basis, but in general whenever I sense a problem, I deal with it quickly. At Inglewood you had to jump on it right away or you'd have a riot in the streets. One example was that every Cinco de Mayo students and outside gang members were out there fighting. The first year I took over we had no fights. I just told the kids, "I'm not having it," and I called the leaders together. I called their parents. We got together with the police chief. A couple of teachers on campus were known to be provokers of the fighting. We got them in that meeting. We met at City Hall.

VALDEZ: The teachers?

MCNALLY: Yes. Most problems that the kids had were started by adults, not by the kids. That was the first year in six years that the school did not have this crazy riot in the middle of the street with kids running around and acting foolishly. It was simply because at the beginning of the year I told them, "I'm not having it. Not on my watch." We talked; we got groups together, and we had the Justice

Department come in. We did some collaborative teaming with the kids. What is it you don't like about each other? Let's sit down and find out, and they found out they weren't mad at each other.

In general, it's important just to deal with it, put it out there and kill the rumor. The first thing you've got to do is kill the rumor because the rumor is what gets the stuff going; it's like wildfire.

VALDEZ: It just goes underground, but you're talking about meeting it head-on with those individuals. They may not do it overtly, but you're talking about a lifetime of conditioning. The views are so ingrained.

MCNALLY: I won't say it can be stopped, but you can put in a stopgap, so they know you're aware. "Mrs. McNally is not going for that," you'll hear the kids and teachers say. If there's an issue, it's not just with the kids; it's an issue among teachers, too, like the issue of separateness. I saw that more at my second high school than at the first. I would go to retirement parties and think, "What happened to the rest of the folks?" Well, they didn't invite them. Then I'd go to another retirement party, and the other folks were missing. I brought this to their attention at the beginning of the year. Like the kids say, "What's up with that? Help me to understand."

I had to force them to be with each other, and we did it through dance. I chose salsa and started at the beginning of the year. They didn't know what we were going to do. I put the conditions out: If you're not able, if you have a medical condition, if it's against your religion, you still need to be in the room. You do not have to physically participate, but I need you there. They didn't know what I was talking about. We went to the cafeteria, and we brought this guy over every Monday who did the salsa movements. They had the best time. You couldn't pair up with your friends. I didn't care if you were female and female. The idea was to get to know each other.

VALDEZ: How much of your meeting time did you do that?

MCNALLY: We did it right before lunch. We took a break at 11:15. It was just an activity, part of staff development. It was staff collaboration. It was getting to know the new teachers. They didn't know these new, young, beautiful teachers from UCLA, who were all by themselves. Do you know what happened? The teachers across town heard about it. "You didn't do that here," they said. I answered, "You're welcome to come over." So, we had salsa dancing from 4-5:30 every Monday.

MORE ON WOMEN OF COLOR

KAWAZOE: *I want to leap to the last question because of time constraints. You mentioned a lot the challenges already, but what are the unique challenges, if any, you've encountered as a woman of color in a highly visible leadership position?*

MOORE: *Maybe you can combine that question with the kind of support you need as a principal.*

DODD: I wasn't expected to last more than six months at McClymonds. It was definitely a male-oriented school. I was the second female administrator and probably the one with the most longevity in terms of just being able to stay there. I went through a lot of naysayers who didn't feel that I was capable of 1) turning around a school and 2) understanding the whole athletic arena. I was expected to allow certain inappropriate actions to occur because a championship was around the corner. I never once agreed because it would jeopardize the school and me. One thing that has helped sustain my longevity is I refuse to allow anybody to move me from my principles and the integrity I hold for my position. I refuse to allow anybody to turn the agenda away from putting students at the top. It's been a long struggle to get adults to understand that the reason that we're here is not because we need a paycheck. It's because we have the job of teaching students who may not have had good experiences prior to coming to McClymonds, but they will have some good experiences before they graduate.

It is an extremely lonely position. I can't tell you how many times I've stayed until 9 or 10 o'clock at night, just trying to figure out if what I'm doing is right, and if I have offended somebody or if I've handled a situation correctly. But I've also learned because it is a lonely position. Even if you have assistant principals and parents and students around you, there is a point when you're on that campus by yourself, and that's when the rubber meets the road. Before I leave the campus, I always try to focus on the good things that happened versus anything that was a negative. That has helped me get over that loneliness, especially when I felt I did not necessarily have a strong support system downtown to rely on. I have had maybe one or two people that I felt I could go to and be very honest with about what was happening at the school and not be put in the position where I was told—and I have had this happen to me—"You will do it this way if you want to keep your job." I began to select those people I felt comfortable with and could tell them what was happening, knowing I could be honest and name names without it going any further. Unfortunately, in Oakland that is not a large pool of people. It's unfortunate that it's turned into everyone for themselves; that's not what I feel the system should be about. We've tried to come up with strong support systems within the school district, but there always seems to be changing leadership at the top.

MCNALLY: I can add a little bit of a spin. I ditto a lot of what Lynn said. But one of the biggest challenges I've had to overcome as a woman of color is that I'm also a woman of color who speaks another language and that blows people away. It's like, "Why is she doing that?" I found that I've gotten the most resistance from people who look like me. Then I get the other from people who don't look like me, "Where did you learn that?" I used to be very defensive: Why did I have to learn it anywhere? Where'd you learn yours? I had to get over that.

We'd go to meetings, and I would sit there on my hands because some poor parent would be struggling, and there was no translator. I knew the moment I opened my mouth, it was going to be, "Oh, yeah, she's just trying to show off." But the parent was struggling, and we didn't make provisions to have a translator. So, I've had to go through that.

In my first assignment as principal I followed a female who had pretty much destroyed the school. Parent rapport was bad. It was the waiting game with the staff. "Oh, how long is she going to be here?" I had taught at that school. I started my teaching career at that school, and some teachers who were there when I was a youngster were now ready to retire. I was treated like I was this little kid, especially from the older men. So I had to assert myself. Then the parents would accuse me of being biased toward one group because I spoke their language.

When I first started, I had excellent support from the superintendent. However, I also found that among other top administrators at the district office there was an attitude that "Oh, that's Ms. McNally. She's so demanding." Whereas Mr. So&So could pick up the phone and say, "I don't have any light bulbs," and he got them within a second. If it were me, I was just being picky. I would have to speak up at meetings. "What are you guys talking about? It's not for me. There are no lights at my house." I would always refer to my school as my house. "Now this house that I manage needs this." I found that I had to fight harder.

I was always being asked to put things in writing when others could walk up and say, "We need 15 more uniforms for the football players or for the band," and my little kids were marching in T-shirts.

The language issue has been with me since I started this profession. I'll never forget my interview at L.A. Unified; that's why I didn't work there initially. I had taken the test, and I'd passed it. They called me for an interview. A lady first said my name wrong, so I didn't answer. You say my name wrong, and I'm not going to answer. My kids are just like that. Finally, she said it three times, and I said, "You know what, excuse me," and I told her my name. She looked at me, and she looked at her papers and said, "These scores I have here, I shouldn't be talking to you" meaning she couldn't figure out how a person like me could get such high scores. The interview panel was mostly men with two women, and they asked me all these questions, and I answered. They asked me to translate something and I did. Then this guy said, "Off the record, where did you learn to speak Spanish like that? I don't even speak it that well, and it's my native tongue." Because I was going for a job I answered him politely, but I wanted to say "You idiot!"

Even now, when I take the mike in front of a group of parents at a town hall meeting, they get really silent if I speak other than English, and the black parents look at me like I'm from another planet. You can't win. But you just press on. I've learned to exercise patience and perseverance. That's what's gotten me through because I get it from both sides. Even when I pronounce my name, they get upset. Ah-dree-ah-na—that's what my mommy calls me.

VALDEZ: I really try to go into work every day as positively as possible. My philosophy is if I made a decision with absolutely no bias in my heart, without setting out to hurt anyone, if I can look anyone in the face and explain why I made the decision, then I'm going to live with that decision. When I make mistakes, I can say I'm sorry and then it'll be ok. The reputation that I have downtown is that I'll do things, and if I do something wrong, then I'll catch heck after the fact. The way I look at things is I need this. This is what my students need; this is what my teachers need; this is what my building needs; and I plan for it. If I have to go back and beg and figure out the additional resources that I need later on, then I'll do that, but the plans are going ahead. If I start planning with just this or that little pot of resources, then I'm going to get the little idea, rather than the big idea. I think the way I'm viewed at the district office is that I'm perhaps too vocal, too honest, too direct.

MCNALLY: Don't forget pushy.

VALDEZ: I pretty much do get what I need in the first call that I make, and that's probably because of my longevity. I have a history in Dinuba. I'm very involved in the community. When you're a leader in the community, you have to be involved, not only in your school, but in the whole community. I have a lot of power because I'm involved in my church, involved in my community, and involved in an administrative position. I'm respected by the people who know me. People who don't know me say, "You're the principal of Dinuba High School?" My color, my youth, being female—all of that, perhaps, causes surprise. Most of the community knows me, so they know who I am and what I'm about. My reputation precedes me. But at meetings and other places, people say with disbelief, "You're principal of a school that size?" I deal with it. I'm my own person. I'm pretty self-assured, and I don't let too much get me down. If I can explain every decision that I make, if I had a good heart in making that decision and students were at the top, then it should be a good decision.

The hardest thing for me was to walk into a school where most teachers were very seasoned with the old mindset about Hispanic students. You know, my husband graduated from that school, and Hispanic students were pretty much moved along. Many teachers did not think that they would go on to college or go on to further education. Some of those mentalities are still there. I always wonder what they think or feel about having a Hispanic female as their principal. It's not something that we necessarily talk about. Again, last year I focused on building relationships and learning about the school, and so I'm looking forward to next year to see what's going to happen.

KAWAZOE: *What about support? You mentioned before that you have the support of your superintendent.*

VALDEZ: Yes, and I want to echo what Lynn said. The most frustrating thing for me has been lack of consistency—when you have one leader, and then another leader, and now another. In our district the history keepers are all gone. There are no history keepers at the district office, other than the principal who left the high school and went on to the district office. But even he doesn't have the district-level history. We're in a precarious position. The interim superintendent is now the superintendent; district office people are finding their identities and their roles. The most frustrating thing for me is that I'm a structure and control person. History and consistency at the district level lead to stability in a small district like ours. When the history is gone, like the domino effect, problems can quickly permeate throughout a small district. In my first year I'd have to say, and the assistant principals would agree, that they had it easy because I knew whom to go to, knew how to get stuff done. I had experienced the challenges with personnel, putting teachers on leave, etc. because I had done that all before, so we just worked through it. But now . . .

KAWAZOE: *Are there any other Hispanic high school principals in the Central Valley?*

VALDEZ: Fresno has a few. There's a female principal in Fresno. Is she still there?

MOORE: *She moved into the district office after a couple of years.*

VALDEZ: That's what happens. But we don't see too many young Hispanic females.

KAWAZOE: *You probably can count them on the fingers of one hand?*

VALDEZ: Yes.

MOORE: *Are there any final thoughts that you might have had about questions that we didn't cover?*

VALDEZ: Time. The biggest challenge is time. I want more time to do everything that I want to do. I want more time to be in the classroom, much more. My staff was shocked at how much I walked. We have a huge campus. I had to get brand new shoes. But I popped into classes as I walked from one end to another, and the teachers were not used to the principal walking through. I stayed for two to three minutes. I told them, "I am your principal; I live in this community. I'm at my son's baseball game here, my other son's soccer game there, this play over here. When parents ask me, I want to be able to speak firsthand about what you're doing in your classroom. I want to be able to tell them how you run your classroom, and the only way I'm going know that is by being in your classroom. So don't feel threatened. I'm not looking for anything negative." I told them right off the bat that my pet peeve is movies. Do not show a movie if it does not pertain to the instruction. You tell me how "School of Rock" pertains to standards.

MCNALLY: This has been a wonderful opportunity for us to collaborate and share ideas. I'm always reflective when I hear others speak about their experiences. It takes me back a bit, and along the way I can put little markers on my own experience. A lot of little "Ah-ha"s came out of this conversation. I'll probably wake up in the middle of the night, and say, "I should have said this. . . ."

VALDEZ: It's the same with teachers. When you get teachers together to talk about student work, a great learning opportunity happens. The same is true for principals. Listening to what we all shared, I'm taking notes on some of the things that I can use.

KAWAZOE: *This conversation highlights the fact that you don't have much chance to talk to your colleagues, whether they're in your district or other districts, about serious issues. So, we might think of places where this could be replicated, where it would be beneficial for both speakers and listeners. It would also be beneficial in principals' leadership training programs.*

MCNALLY: I'll tell you where I'm going to take it. I'm going to share this experience with my superintendent. We meet religiously the first and third Wednesdays with our principals, and we always have meetings in the afternoon where we break out into secondary and elementary sections. If there were some good guiding questions—like the ones you provided for us—some good conversations could take place, because you're right, we don't have a chance to talk to each other, especially in a big district. Our principals have been asking for it. They do get a chance to meet, but they're always listening to somebody else; they don't hear their own voices.

KAWAZOE: *In a given district, there can be different ways to lead a school that will effectively move the school forward. There isn't necessarily one prescribed way that's going to be the right way, but leaders need to find their own way.*

MCNALLY: The most egregious thing we all talked about and that I see happening with new principals or principals in new positions is that they always assume they have to change everything. But that just messes up the scenario. Don't change much that first year, but come in and find out and listen and take notes.

VALDEZ: The district office personnel need to make that clear to new administrators.

DODD: Make it clear, but also allow the person that they are asking to assume those responsibilities some freedom and power to own what's going to happen with that school.

MCNALLY: One issue that emerged in our conversation was our leadership styles. Listening to everyone around the table, I didn't hear anyone say, "I'm autocratic or whatever." I heard of a more eclectic, supportive, open-door, listener style, the kind of leadership style that's hard to label.

VALDEZ: It's a little bit of all the different styles, depending on the situation. In some situations you may be a dictator because that's what you need at that time.

DODD: Your personality changes to suit the situation.

KAWAZOE: *That's part of developing smartness, to know when to be autocratic when decisions have to be made and you're the one to make them, and when to be democratic.*

MCNALLY: I used to tell my staff that discussion is good. I appreciate your input, but you do understand that in some cases I will have to make the final decision. I remember the first time I said that someone replied, "What does that mean?" I was quick on the draw, sometimes too quick, and said, "What do you think it means?" and I thought, "Oops! Wrong answer." But it was out there. Whether it was good or bad, I realized we're all just human beings. We're having a good discussion, a necessary discussion. They're taking notes, and I'm collecting the charts, but they need to realize that I will have to take all this into account and make the final decision. "That's what I mean!" I said.

❖ ❖ ❖

Commentary

ALICE KAWAZOE

Earth, air, fire, and water—the four elements of the universe, so the ancients say. Lynn Dodd, Adriana McNally, and Yolanda Valdez are clearly women of fire. Their passion and commitment to educating all students light up this dialogue. Though they may suffer at times from doubts and frustrations, these no-nonsense, assertive women are forces to be reckoned with as they set high performance standards for themselves and their staffs, make difficult decisions, and generally take charge of their schools.

Like many of their students, the women suffered from negative labeling and preconceived notions of their potential. Yolanda, from a migrant worker family, remembers she was "made to sit down, look forward, and do the work," and a high school counselor who would not enroll her in college prep English assigned her to Business English instead. Feisty even then, Yolanda replied, "Okay, go ahead . . . I'm going to college anyway." Lynn recalls being "pigeonholed to learn and respond in a certain way," so that she "became arrogant, militant." She was frustrated by "a system that had and still has a lot of racial overtones that keep minority students from graduating." Adriana cites the over-identification of African American males in special education as evidence of continued pigeonholing. "We think there is a certain place some students should occupy." These African American males "are intelligent, but because no one has heard them, they tend to strike out a lot and get in trouble."

Fortunately, each of these women leaders benefited from at least one person who motivated and encouraged them. For Yolanda, it was a migrant counselor who made her believe she "could have the world." Adriana declares "Supervisors have always prodded me," and Lynn recalls fondly a librarian who saw something in her that made her "at least think about education." These women know the power of a positive advocate and have not forgotten the importance of advocacy and commitment to underserved students—Yolanda for English learners "who don't have the luxury of time" to gain fluency in English and succeed in classes; Adriana for students who are written off, as one such student declared, "Everybody automatically assumes that I'm not going anywhere, that I can't do anything"; and Lynn for special education students and for other students who are deemed "not capable of learning."

Perhaps because of their personal histories and backgrounds, all three women understand the moral purpose of education. They have little patience for incompetence at any level, and recalcitrant teachers who shun improvement earn their special professional animosity. The women express righteous indignation about teachers who do not take charge of teaching or take responsibility for educating students.

In response to the common practice of blaming the learner by saying, "Oh, the kid is the problem," Adriana tosses the onus for learning back to teachers: ". . . the kids are not supposed to be harassing you. You're supposed to harass the kids—in a positive way—in that you have so much going on for them that they don't have the time to think about not doing it." Lynn explodes when she sees pervasive low levels of expectations and teaching at her school, and few staff willing to take responsibility: "How can you justify constantly creating documents that have a human being attached to them where you are not elevating the expectations? Is that your level of teaching competency? Can't you teach beyond this low level? If that's the case, then we don't need you here."

An extension of the moral purpose of education is the reality that high schools are often the hearts of the community or town. They are the centers of activities that unite the community; they are safe sanctuaries for students against the dangers of the outside world. Each principal embraces and is embraced by the families and community. Yolanda was born and raised in the community, and she has chosen to live and raise her family there. She serves as both an educational and civic leader. Adriana and Lynn know their communities from long experience and interaction. Lynn fights the district against closure and for survival of her school in west Oakland by establishing a community health center on campus. Adriana recruits the help of businesses and families to host the Academic Decathlon, not just to change the image of the school, but to alter the mindsets of students, staff, and community about the school as an academic, as well as athletic, power.

With storytelling and pointed examples, honesty, and dashes of humor, the women spend much of the dialogue discussing the issues of high school improvement: collaboration, using data, creating a positive school culture, establishing credibility with staff, making changes, building teaching and leadership capacity, maintaining and sustaining leadership, and administrative training programs. When asked about racism, the women discuss how they deal with racism at their schools, not about the possible racism in their professional careers. One of Yolanda's comments, "Having low expectations of students is a kind of racism," deserves more discussion, but the talk takes another direction.

After listening to these three women leaders talk and savoring their stories, transcribing and editing their conversation, and reading their words, several questions loom large. What if Yolanda Valdez, Adriana

McNally, and Lynn Dodd were not women of color? Would they be as passionate and committed to their students? To say that they would not, would imply that paler principals, principals not of color, are not as passionate about their profession and are less committed to their students, and that is clearly untrue. But as we often say that students benefit from role models, adults "who look like them," so, too, the converse may be true: we feel strong connection and obligation to students who look like younger versions of ourselves. We see ourselves in them; we know them. We feel deeply the moral imperative to give them hope and a path to success.

Shortly after reading a draft of the dialogue and long after the actual exhilarating experience, Nina Moore and I were surprised that more issues of women of color did not surface more overtly. But these women do not view the world, and the world does not view them, through a single lens. Gender, ethnicity, language, age, leadership, power, and values are just a few of the lenses available to people, and most times we view an experience through multiple lenses. Lynn talks about the gender battles with African American male administrators. Adriana mentions her Spanish-speaking abilities as an issue. Youth and outspokenness become issues with Yolanda. Further, experiences are complex with multiple causes, consequences, motives, and implications, sometimes difficult to detect. For example, to see racism in every major act is a not a result of rational analysis, but a sign of psychosis. These three women are not psychotic, and they do not have the time to analyze each incident or experience. They are too busy acting, doing. Perhaps sometime in the near future, we can reunite the women and probe the issue of women of color more deeply.

And just a few words about conversation and writing. This conversation, although guided by questions, was free-flowing and spontaneous, characterized by the ebb and flow of three women talking—one story leading to another, wandering to another idea, changing topics, circling back to a previous notion, injecting sarcasm, and laughing. Some people may become irritated by this "organic" talk, with little extending ideas, drawing implications, thinking through to logical conclusions that writing affords. Nina Moore and I opted for spontaneity and immediacy when we decided to bring the women together to talk, rather than write an exposition. Even in converting the talk to written form, we have sacrificed some of the dynamism, enthusiasm, and fervor we experienced that day.

I earlier characterized Lynn Dodd, Adriana McNally, and Yolanda

Valdez as women of fire. None is submissive, bland, inconsequential, quiet, or wimpy. They are the exact opposite: assertive, bold, powerful, outspoken, and nervy. They are incendiary leaders. I am reminded of a slogan I heard a long while ago: "A burned-out teacher was once a teacher on fire." Perhaps that is what our weary, burned-out high schools need most desperately: someone to light them up and reignite the passion for teaching, commitment to students, and moral purpose of education. They need someone like Lynn Dodd, Adriana McNally, and Yolanda Valdez.

❖ ❖ ❖

Commentary

NINA MOORE

In getting ready for this dialogue with the three principals, Alice Kawazoe and I prepared two pages of questions. We did not expect to cover each one; rather we intended to use them as a guide to spark a conversation. I remember the five hours we spent with these three dynamic women and how little we needed any kind of prompt for their dialogue with one another. It was such a privilege to listen to the conversation, to have a window into their experiences and, in many ways, into their hearts, minds, and souls.

Reading this "case study" in retrospect, the written words do not fully capture the essence of the interaction we were so privileged to experience. However, they do illustrate the depth and range of issues educational leaders face on a daily basis. At one point in the conversation, the women talked about sustaining the work and best practices that they were able to put in place through the inevitable leadership changes. It is clear that leadership instability in schools and districts takes a toll on sustaining improvement, morale, and best practices. But all three of these leaders suggested that it is important to put systems in place and build capacity so that effective changes are not dismantled if a principal or other leader leaves. As Adriana McNally said, ". . . *it's not about the person; it's about the system and the services that have been put in place. . . ."*

Yet when I read about the experiences each of the principals shared, what they did at their schools has everything to do with who they are as individuals. It has to do with really seeing the children, the teachers, the other staff, the families, and the communities as individual gifts contributing to a whole school family. They talked about attending to the whole child, his or her life circumstances, health needs, and social needs, as well as academics. This is also true for how they viewed their teaching staff, fellow administrators, and other adults in the school community. Is it possible to have a "system" that can address the complexity of this kind of human organization? I believe that systems are necessary but not sufficient in education. It is clear to me that the person, the leader who is ultimately responsible for the school, is critical to creating an environment that nurtures, sustains, and encourages the best in each member of the community.

So, are educational leaders born or can they be trained? This question for me remains unanswered. While each of the women learned important administrative skills in their respective preparation programs, all felt much of the most important learning took place on the job. My sense is that the most important qualities they bring to their work as educators—creativity, empathy, commitment, passion, strength, quick and agile thinking, patience, perseverance, and a sense of moral purpose—are not ones learned from a textbook.

As the title and introduction to the dialogue suggest, we were also interested in learning about whether being women of color posed any unique challenges or opportunities for these three leaders. In reading the case study, this issue does not seems as important as I remember it being from our discussion. While there are certainly references to their experiences as women of color, race did not seem to emerge as a central theme. I suppose *my* memory is colored by sitting in the room with these women and seeing two African American women and one Hispanic woman. Are their challenges the same as any other educational leader? I wonder if the issue was not explicit because they simply move through the world as who they are with the knowledge that color is just part of how they move and respond. There was a conversation about having to do more than some other people and a sense of loneliness being a woman of color in a leadership position. I wonder if it is not more explicit because women of color just expect to work twice as hard and rely on themselves, where others may have a stronger professional support system. I wonder if race and gender informs all of the work women of color do, both our own as well as others' perceptions of us.

After listening to the dialogue live and reading the case study in print, I still wonder about some of the issues that emerged and some that did not. Not all of my questions were answered. But I am enormously grateful to have been part of this important and insightful dialogue. The honesty, commitment, passion, and strength of Lynn Dodd, Adriana McNally, and Yolanda Valdez are a gift to the students, teachers, administrators, and families in California. I am honored to have the opportunity to work with these three women of color and know that the gifts they bring are unique.

Contributors

Judy Bebelaar was an English teacher in the San Francisco Unified School District.

Marge Chisholm was on the California Post-Secondary Education Commission (CPEC).

Katrine Czajkowski is a teacher and project director at Mar Vista High School, Imperial Beach, California.

Lynn Dodd was an administrator in the Oakland Unified School District in California and is currently at the College Board.

Leo Florendo is a physics teacher at Woodside High School in Woodside, California.

Zelda Glazer was Director of English Language Arts for the Miami/Dade County School District.

Kate Jamentz is the Assistant Superintendent of Curriculum for the Fremont High School District in Cupertino, California.

Dave Jolly is Director of the California Academic Partnership Program (CAPP).

Michelle Kalina is Senior Director for Operations of California Partnership for Achieving Student Success (Cal-PASS).

Alice Kawazoe was a teacher and administrator and is currently a consultant for the California Academic Partnership Program (CAPP).

Ed Landesman is Professor Emeritus of Mathematics at the University of California, Santa Cruz.

Adriana McNally was a principal in Inglewood School District and is currently Director of School Services in the Los Angeles Unified School District, Local District 7.

Nina Moore is at the University of California, Office of the President and California Academic Partnership Program (CAPP) consultant.

Adam Randall is a mathematics teacher at Woodside High School in Woodside, California.

Lorie Roth is Vice Chancellor of the California State University system.

Yolanda Valdez is the Principal at Dinuba High School in Dinuba, California.

Jon Wagner is Professor of Education at the University of California, Davis.

Alan Weisberg was a teacher and administrator and is currently a consultant for the California Academic Partnership Program (CAPP).

Barbara Wells taught mathematics at the secondary and college levels and currently provides professional development support for the California Academic Partnership Program (CAPP).

Printed in the United States
154455LV00001B/2/P

9 780615 277318